T5-AVM-907

DISCRETIONARY MANAGERIAL BEHAVIOR

DISCRETIONARY MANAGERIAL BEHAVIOR

by

T.V.S. RAMAMOHAN RAO
Indian Institute of Technology - Kanpur

and

RANJUL RASTOGI
Society for Capital Market Research and Development - New Delhi

KLUWER ACADEMIC PUBLISHERS
BOSTON / DORDRECHT / LONDON

A C.I.P. Catalogue record for this book is available from the Library of Congress.

ISBN 0-7923-8016-9

Published by Kluwer Academic Publishers,
P.O. Box 17, 3300 AA Dordrecht, The Netherlands.

Sold and distributed in the U.S.A. and Canada
by Kluwer Academic Publishers,
101 Philip Drive, Norwell, MA 02061, U.S.A.

In all other countries, sold and distributed
by Kluwer Academic Publishers,
P.O. Box 322, 3300 AH Dordrecht, The Netherlands.

Printed on acid-free paper

Printed in the Netherlands.

About the book

Information asymmetry and the resulting adverse selection and moral hazard are intrinsic to every decentralized organization. The managers at every level of the organization experience these problems in their decision making process. In particular, the managers at the divisional levels are never in a position to assess their contribution to the overall objectives of the firm. As a consequence the higher level management generally expects them to pursue certain proximate objectives. The divisional managers, in their turn, operate under such constraints but find it necessary and feasible to pursue personal objectives. Such objectives may include a preference for harmonious relations with the divisional workforce, prestige associated with large size, and the degree of control they exercise. The theoretical literature of organizational economics has not come to grips with the decision making process in such organizations. Instead, a vast amount of research is directed to an analysis of the efficiency of the functioning of the internal capital markets in a M-form organization. The present study is an attempt to model the objectives of the management while making the long term investment decisions, the decisions of the marketing manager, and the choices of the production manager in the short run.

The basic premise is that each of the divisional managers has a well defined objective, can assess the environment - external to the division and the firm - in which the decisions must be made, and the constraints imposed by the higher level controller. A new approach to modelling was developed because the existing formulations could not reflect the realities of the choices adequately.

The identification of the parameters of such optimization models was also a formidable task. A fundamentally new approach to the identification of such models was therefore developed.

The empirical analysis of 27 firms in the chemical industry confirmed that useful information about managerial choices in decentralized organizations can be obtained by utilizing such a modelling framework. In particular, the following results should be highlighted. While making the long term investment decisions the managers express a preference either for the growth of capital assets or the control implied by the debt equity ratio. They are, however, averse to taking the risks of financing excessive growth by a high debt equity ratio. That is, the bonding effects are significant even if there is an element of discretion in the long term choices of the management. Turning to the marketing managers, they have a tendency to target a lower than profit maximizing level of market share and indulge in excessive selling costs. In contrast to the existing studies, which emphasize the market structure as the major source of excessive advertising, such a behavior of the management in decentralized organizations is independent of the nature of the product market. Similarly, the more realistic objective for the production manager is to choose the personnel and inventory policies to fulfill the sales targets set by the marketing manager. Inventories will then be mostly precautionary and tend to be excessive if the management is risk averse.

Clearly this study represents a modest beginning to the quantification of the managerial behavior within decentralized organizations. However, this approach can be expected to provide practical insights into the internal functioning of the firm, the relationships between the managers at different organizational echelons, and the conditioning effects of organizational controls and the market environment external to the firm. The relevance of such studies to business policy is the fundamental justification for the development of microeconomics along these lines in the near future.

About the authors

Educated at the Indian Statistical Institute and the University of Southern California, Los Angeles, Dr.Rao has been a professor of economics at the Indian Institute of Technology, Kanpur since 1978. Before joining the Indian Institute of Technology, Kanpur he taught at the California State University, Long Beach and the Kansas State University, Manhattan. He was also a visiting professor at the University of Pennsylvania, Philadelphia and the University of Alberta, Edmonton. Dr.Rao has published extensively, on both economic theory and applied econometrics, in international as well as Indian journals. His current research interests include organizational economics and strategic management.

Dr.Rastogi received her Ph.D from the Indian Institute of Technology, Kanpur. She also has degrees in economics and law from Allahabad University. Dr.Rastogi was a lecturer at the Indian Institute of Finance, New Delhi during 1996. She is currently a senior research associate at the Society for Capital Market Research and Development, New Delhi. She is an expert in corporate finance and has publications in both international and Indian journals. Her current research interest is in the developments in the bond markets.

PREFACE

The typical modern corporation has three characteristics.

(a) It operates in an uncertain market environment. This necessitates product as well as portfolio diversification. Largeness of size and diffused ownership, with its implications for limited liability, are the distinct features of such a firm.

(b) The large size and the consequent information requirements for decision making necessitate a decentralized organizational structure. The management operates under delegated responsibility and they can at best have limited property rights resulting from their shareholding. Clearly their motivations in the decision making process can be different from those of the owners. Knight (1933, p.22) noted that cooperation and subgroup compliance can be achieved only if the organizational objective is compromised while accommodating the aspirations of the divisional managers.

(c) The owners of the firm are mostly the shareholders and the term lending institutions. As Berle and Means (1932) argued, none of the individual stakeholders is large enough to have an interest in controlling the firm. Instead, they prefer to free ride on the decisions of the others. This gives rise to the possibility that the management gains control over the decision making of the corporation.

For all practical purposes it can be argued that managerial discretion is ubiquitous.

However, both the theoretical and empirical attempts to systematize this aspect of the behavior of the firm have not been successful. There are two essential dimensions of this problem.

(a) The very notion that the management has discretion suggests that they pursue multiple goals rather than a single objective like the maximization of profits or the market value of the firm. The theoretical speculation on the possible objectives is very rich. The prominent analytical arguments include Baumol (1959), Cyert and March (1963), Williamson (1964), Marris(1964), Leibenstein (1980), Hoenack (1983), and Grossman and Hart (1982). Yarrow (1973; 1976,p.267) stated the fundamental problem. As he puts it, "once managerial discretion is allowed, economic theory has little to say about the components and shapes of managerial utility functions". In particular, as Lintner (1971, p.218) suggested, it has not been possible to conceptualize "the relative weights to be given to equity-value increasing objectives and other elements in the utility function of business as they affect and determine actual decision situations." This has led Yarrow (1976, p.267) to argue that the "best that can be done is to hypothesize a particular type of objective function, explore its consequences, and where possible, test (the consequences of) the model against the evidence." There are fundamental estimation problems even if this approach is accepted. For, as Schmalensee (1989, p.957) pointed out, the "data on endogenous variables (i.e., the actual decisions of the management) do provide information, though not the sort that can be handled by commonly employed estimation techniques." Radice (1971, p.549) and Cubbin and Leech (1986, p.124) also recognized the existence of an identification problem that must be resolved.

(b) There is as yet no clear description of the objectives that each of the decentralized divisions within the firm pursue. However, it has been acknowledged that none of the divisions can directly know their contribution to the overall profits of the firm except in certain specific types of organizations. Profit maximization as the proximate objective of every division is operationally infeasible. The alternatives are not easy to conceptualize let alone make them analytically tractable. As Barney (1986, p.141) put it, "until organization- economic concepts are more fully developed in explaining (the behavior within the firms) they will be of less utility in organization theory than was anticipated." It is necessary to make some progress in this direction both analytically and empirically.

With this in perspective the present study attempts to examine the following three aspects of the problem.

(a) As a first step, efforts have been made to identify the proximate objectives of the management of the different divisions of the firm. This approach is superior to the assumption that there is a common goal for all the divisions of the enterprise.

For, none of the divisional managers can be expected to know enough about the effects of their decisions on the overall objective of the firm if there is any.

(b) A simple estimation method, based on the fundamental economic reasoning underlying the decision making process, has been developed. This basic contribution to the resolution of the identification problem made it possible to undertake a meaningful empirical study.

(c) The estimates for several firms in the chemical industry have been developed to provide better insights into the managerial decision making process at the divisional level of decentralized organizations.

As such this study is a first step, albeit an important one, to make fundamental progress in this area of interface between business policy and microeconomic theory.

During the course of this work we had the benefit of observations from various individuals. In particular, R.R.Barthwal helped us in rethinking about some aspects of the specification as well as measurement. The large amount of computing time that we needed was generously provided by the IIT, Kanpur. We record our appreciation.

We are also thankful to Allard Winterink of the Kluwer Academic Publishers for the efficient and thoughtful processing of our manuscript.

T.V.S.Ramamohan Rao
Ranjul Rastogi

CONTENTS

LIST OF FIRMS

1. ALB - Albright, Morarji and Pandit Ltd
2. ALEM - Alembic Chemical Works Company Ltd
3. ARL - Arlabs Ltd
4. BASF - BASF India Ltd
5. BAYER - Bayer (India) Ltd
6. BOOTS - Boots Pharmaceuticals Ltd
7. BORAX - Borax Morarji Ltd
8. COCHIN - Cochin Refineries Ltd
9. COLOR - Color Chemicals Ltd
10. CORO - Coromandel Fertilizers Ltd
11. DCW - DCW Ltd
12. DHM - Dharamsi Morarji Chemical Company Ltd
13. DYES - Dyestuffs Industries (India) Ltd
14. GLAXO - Glaxo Ltd
15. GUJ - Gujarat State Fertilizers Company Ltd
16. HERDIL - Herdillia Chemicals Ltd
17. IDL - IDL Chemicals Ltd
18. JLM - J.L.Morrisons (India) Ltd
19. KANOR - Kanoria Chemical Industries Ltd
20. NOCIL - National Organic Chemical Industries Ltd
21. POLY - Polyolefins Industries Ltd
22. RALLIS - Rallis India Ltd
23. SANDOZ - Sandoz (India) Ltd
24. SYNTH - Synthetics and Chemicals Ltd
25. TATA - Tata Chemicals Ltd
26. UNICHEM - Unichem Laboratories Ltd
27. UNION - Union Carbide of India Ltd

LIST OF FIRMS

1. [illegible]
3. [illegible]
4. [illegible]
11. [illegible]
20. [illegible]
21. [illegible] Industries Ltd
22. [illegible]
23. [illegible]
24. [illegible]
25. [illegible]
26. [illegible]
27. [illegible]

LIST OF VARIABLES

MAVA - Market Value of the firm

NPRO - Net Profits

NSAL - Net Sales

GRTH - Growth Rate of Capital Assets

DEBT - Debt Equity Ratio

GNEX - Advertising Intensity

INSA - Inventory to Sales Ratio

WASA - Wages and Salaries to Cost of Goods Sold

NFAS - Net Fixed Assets

BSRI - Business Risk

FIRI - Financial Risk

TAXT - Provision for Taxation

LIQD - Liquidity Ratio

DIND - Dividends per Share

LIST OF FIGURES

LIST OF TABLES

SOURCES OF MANAGERIAL DISCRETION

1.1. Managerial Discretion

The management literature emphasizes one of two objectives of firms in the corporate sector :

(a) maximization of short run profits, or

(b) maximization of the market value of the firm in the long run.

In practice it is not possible to aim at

(a) both these goals simultaneously, or

(b) either of these goals and neglect the stability of the market share of the firm or its future prospects.

For instance, suppose the management is aware of a new market prospect or developed a new product through R&D efforts. It will be advantageous in the long run to incorporate such opportunities in the production lines of the firm. This necessitates committing finances in the short run though

(a) the returns will accrue only with a time lag, and

(b) there is always some uncertainty associated with such investments.

A notion of maximizing profit and/or market value at each point of time is impractical.

When the corporate entity is taken to be an ongoing enterprise it would be far more reasonable to postulate that such maximization will be constrained by

(a) the distinctive competencies of the firm[1],

---

1. According to Hitt and Ireland (1986, p.402) a "distinctive competence is a firm's ability to complete an action in a manner superior to that of its competitors or to apply a skill that competitors lack." Such distinctive competencies can be found in functional areas, e.g., personnel, production, marketing, finance, and so on. An exhaustive treatment of the effects of distinctive competencies on corporate strategy and success can be found in Kay (1995).

(b) the requirements of market share stability, and
(c) the prospects of growth within manageable limits. See, for example, Marris (1964).
Clearly, the number of constraints which enter the decision making process can be quite large.

The theoretical efficiency arguments, which make a number of abstract assumptions, impute a certain degree of inefficiency with such decision making processes. The expression, managerial discretion, which is basically an acknowledgement of the tendency to trade off profit or market value to pursue other objectives, has been used pejoratively.

However, such concepts of inefficiency have been contested. See, for instance, DeAlessi (1983) and Gravelle (1982). In the extreme form the argument is that the corporate objectives can be defined only by taking into account the aspirations and idiosyncracies of all the individuals who participate in the activities of the enterprise[2].

---

2. On occasions it is pointed out that even the shareholders may not be interested in profit or value maximization. For, in general, they consider
(a) the short run gains in the form of dividend payments, and
(b) the capital gains which can be expected in the long run.
Clearly, a large profit during any interval of time contributes to enhancing the attainment of their objective. However, it is not possible to argue that no other factor can influence the expected capital gains. In particular,
(a) an appropriate strategy of product diversification,
(b) an increase in market share, and
(c) a perception regarding the managerial motivations and performance can influence the share prices and capital gains.
In otherwords, even the shareholders may have multiple goals and assign different weights to each of them. It would be difficult to assign a normative role to value maximization since the shareholder objectives are not clearly articulated.

Even this approach has not been useful in providing an insight into
(a) the various aspects which the management considers in the decision making process, and
(b) the relative weights assigned to different objectives.
Hence, the study of managerial discretion should attempt to obtain information about these aspects. Stated in these terms the problem is open ended and hence analytically intractable[3].

The best that can be done is to
(a) seek information about a few salient aspects,
(b) update knowledge periodically, and
(c) acknowledge that certain conceptual and/or methodological judgements should be reviewed periodically.

1.2. Market Structure

It can be shown that the market imperfection is itself one of the sources of managerial discretion. This can manifest itself in several forms. Only a few salient features will be presented in this section.

In the contemporary industrial setting most of the firms derive market advantages by exploiting the economies of scale inherent in the production of their primary product. This was eminently documented in Chandler (1962,1990). Given the technologically determined economies of scale and the limits of the domestic market for their product only a few firms can establish themselves in the market. This results in an oligopolistic market organization. A natural urge on the part of the owner managers would be to explore wide ranging geographical markets, including those overseas, to take advantage of the scale economies. Chandler (1990) documented this managerial attitude as well. Firms tend to expand and consolidate their market dominance and market share even when there are diminishing returns to such activity.

---

3. Further, there may be a certain inherent dynamics in these managerial motivations. This will be difficult to disentangle.

Due to the monopolistic or oligopolistic nature of the product market it can be argued that the results of their decisions and their performance depend on the actions and reactions of the rival firms. However, it is often assumed that most of the firms ignore these competitive interrelationships by creating a niche for themselves in their market segment. See, for instance, Chamberlin (1962) and Hart (1985). The brand loyalty they can create in this manner complements the scale effects in reducing the elasticity of demand for their products and enabling them to make some short run profits. The notion that enhancing and/or stabilizing the market share is an important objective of the owner-manager of the firm suggests that the manager would utilize these short run profits to create and/or strengthen the niche segments of the market for their products along with the profit maximizing goals. The manager has a discretion in the allocation of resources to these two activities.

Consider Fig. 1.1. Let S be the volume of sales and π be the

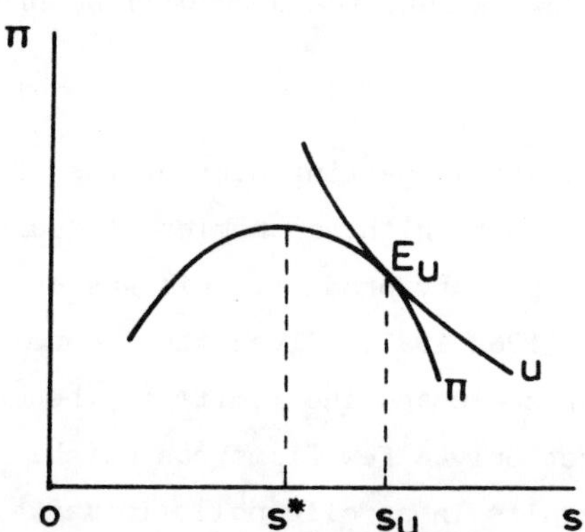

FIG. 1.1. PREFERENCE FOR MARKET SHARE

profits of the firm. The demand curve for the firm is

p = price per unit of sales

$= f(S)\ ;\ f_1 < 0$

where f_1 is the derivative of f with respect to S.

Hence, the profit function

$\pi = \pi(S)$

is of the inverted U-shape. A profit maximizing firm would choose S^*. However, if the managerial preference is towards stabilizing market share as represented by

Maximize $U = U(\pi, S)$; $U_1, U_2 > 0$

then $S_u > S^*$ will be the actual choice of the management. This is the essential implication of discretionary managerial behavior.

Implicit in the above argument is the acknowledgement that competing with other firms, rather than seeking a niche, may involve greater uncertainty and variability of earnings even if the profits increase on an average. A risk averse manager may prefer to reduce the variability of earnings even if this results in a lower average profit. This is another aspect of managerial discretion. Refer to Fig. 1.2.

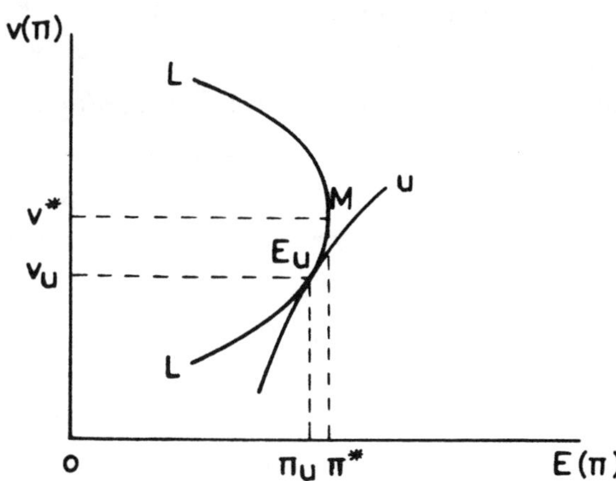

FIG.1.2. RISK AVERSION

Let the demand curve be

$p = f(S) + u$

where u is a random variable with

$E(u) = 0$, and $V(u) = \sigma^2$

where E(u) and V(u) are respectively the expected value and the variance of u.

Note that as S increases the expected value (E) of profit increases initially, reaches a maximum and decreases thereafter. However, $V(\pi)$ increases monotonically with S. The locus of the (V,E) combinations obtained by eliminating S from these can be represented as LL. If the management is risk averse, that is,

$U = U(E,V)$; $U_1 > 0$, $U_2 < 0$

then the optimal choice of S will be at the point E_u rather than M. The implication of this managerial discretion is that they will agree to $\pi_u < \pi^*$ to achieve $V_u < V^*$.

In general, as Hicks (1935) observed, the best of all monopoly profits may be quiet life in the sense that there is a preference for a greater stability of market share even if the level of profits is not the maximum at every point of time.

When confronted with business risk[4] a wide range of policies, not necessarily increasing S, may be pursued by the management in its endeavor to maintain the operations of the firm at an even keel. This will be pursued further in the sequel.

A similar argument holds even in the context of acquisition of inputs. For, it may be more economical to enter into a contract for a steady supply even at a higher price rather than be subjected to market fluctuations from one time period to the next. See, for instance, Carleton (1978).

1.3. Product Diversification

As Chandler (1962,1990) remarked, the possibilities of expanding markets for any given product line encounter diminishing returns sooner than later. The management would then undertake diversification into related activities which can increase the utilization of its capital equipment. Such a product

---

4. Turnovsky (1970, p.1064) and Vickers (1987,pp.162-3) distinguish between business risk and financial risk. They characterize business risk as a situation in which the demand for the different products of the firm is uncertain. On the other hand, financial risk represents the interest payments and repayment liabilities of utilizing debt to finance the capital assets of the firm.

diversification can have an effect on the demand for the firm's products as well as spread the costs over them. See, for example, Clemens (1951, p.8) and Glete (1989)[5]. The first stage of development of the firm is usually value addition by forward vertical integration.

Consider a firm which is currently producing steel ingots. Clearly it is an intermediate product which requires further processing before there can be any end use to the consumer. In particular, it is necessary to process it into wires, plates and so on to add value to it. Similarly, a manufacturer of personal computers can increase the market for its products by expanding into the production of specific software which will make the PC more valuable to the final user. The firms can generate greater profits and/or market value by expanding into such value adding activities. Consider Fig. 1.3. Let D_n be the demand curve for the

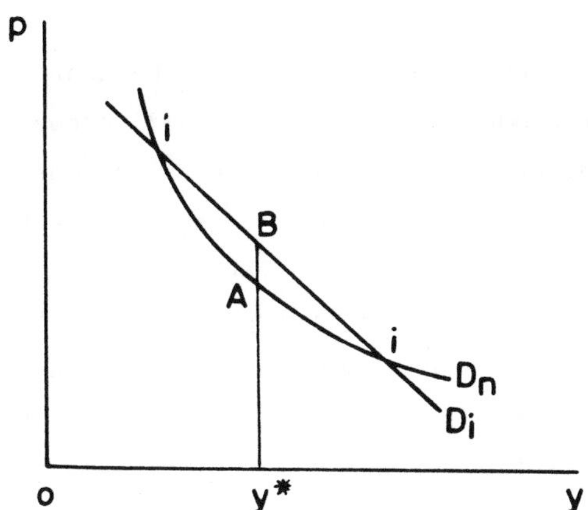

FIG.1.3. FORWARD INTEGRATION

products of the firm prior to forward integration. It can be

---

5. This is best reflected by the following quotation from Young (1928, p.536)- "the search for markets is not a matter of disposing of a 'surplus product,' ... but of finding an outlet for a potential product. Nor is it wholly a matter of multiplying profits by multiplying sales; it is partly a matter of augmenting c fits by reducing costs."

expected that the value addition will shift the demand curve to D_i. In particular, when the output Y is low it may not be able to derive any advantages due to the limited market for the specific value addition that it undertakes. Similarly, when the output is fairly large competitors will try to duplicate the products and reduce the specificity of the firm's product. In general, value addition may be beneficial between the points marked as i. Then, for a given level of Y^*, value addition increases the price per unit of output by an amount AB. The technological and organizational capabilities define the limits on AB. However, the managements of certain firms may decide to stop short of the maximum AB that can be achieved. Clearly, there are several dynamic considerations which limit the managers from aiming at the value addition implied by D_i and/or the output Y^*. The major reason why the managers exercise this discretion is a subjective assessment of the future prospects and the extent of competitive response.

A parallel argument reflects the possibility of backward vertical integration into input production. As Coase (1937) argued, the necessity for such a diversification decision arises due to the transaction costs of input acquisition through the market interface[6]. The existence of excess capacity, which is characteristic of firms operating in such product markets, is usually the enabling factor. For, some fixed capital can be shared by the output as well as the input. However, backward vertical integration may be justifiable even with increasing marginal costs so long as the transaction costs are fairly large.

Suppose the firm decides to produce one of the inputs, say I, internally. Then, referring to Fig.1.4, adapted from Rao (1989, p.56), AC_m represents the average cost of producing a given level of output Y when production is organized by purchasing the input

---

6. The argument holds even if the firm is currently obtaining its inputs through a long term contract. For a detailed analysis see Rao (1993).

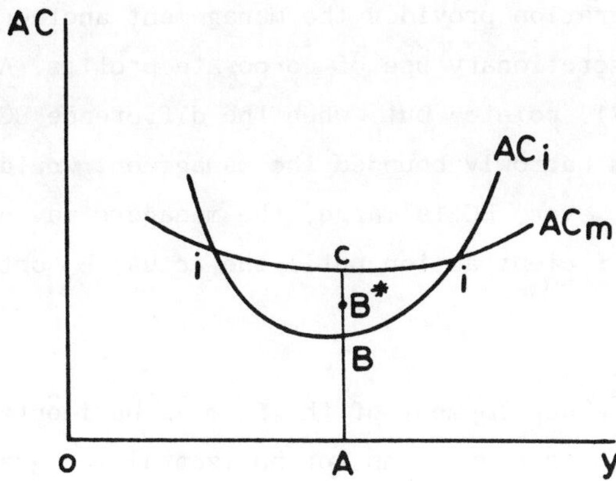

FIG. 1.4. VERTICAL INTEGRATION

from the market and AC_i the average cost when I is produced within the firm. Backward vertical integration is then beneficial between the points marked as i. For, assume that A is the volume of output produced. AC is the average cost if the inputs are purchased on the market. AB is the minimum possible cost if the production of I is internalized. The positive difference BC in the cost is the primary motivation for the internalization of the production of I.

The actual level of costs, which can be obtained for the given level of output A, will generally exceed the minimum AB possible. For, note that

(a) the management may not have any objective way of apportioning the fixed costs between Y and I to determine the appropriate price per unit of I[7], and

(b) the consolidated profit and loss account of the firm does not readily reveal to the shareholders the transfer price which the management imputes for a unit of the input.

---

7. This also suggests that neither the incumbent firms in the market nor the potential competitors have any accurate way of assessing the profitability of the product market. This barrier to entry may increase the inelasticity of demand, the profits of the firm, and the potential for managerial discretion. See Bates and Parkinson (1982, pp. 304 ff).

Hence, backward integration provides the management another dimension for the discretionary use of corporate profits. As Williamson (1964, p.11) pointed out, when the difference BC is small and survival is narrowly bounded the management would approximate B. If, however, BC is large, the managers may not be forced to initiate efficient action until the actual B^* obtained approaches C.

The third stage in the development of the firm is horizontal integration. One of the explanations for horizontal integration relates to the nature of technology and the associated cost structure. In certain product lines the basic technology is quite complex and involves the installation of extensive assembly lines. However, in the early phases of the operating cycle of any primary product the demand for it may be low, even if it is sustainable in the sense that it generates positive profit, thereby causing excess capacity. Hence, the fixed costs are initially shared by a few units of output. The profit position of the firm can be improved if it is possible to utilize the fixed capacity and spread the fixed costs over a related product.

Baumol et al (1982) extended this argument to take even the variable factors into account. For, it was suggested that the technology of production may offer significant economies of scope. Similarly, Sharkey (1982) identified the possibilities of specific organizational capabilities as well. To illustrate this viewpoint consider the possibility that an M-form organization emerges in the multiproduct setting. In such a case, as Teece (1980, p.232) noted, there can be certain transaction cost advantages. For, " internal trading changes the incentives of the parties and enables the firm to bring certain managerial control devices to bear on the transaction, thereby attenuating costly haggling and disruptions and other manifestations of non-cooperative behavior. Exchange can then proceed at a lower cost."

One further possibility was identified by Bates and Parkinson (1982, pp.305 ff). During certain intervals of time the management of the firm may perceive an opportunity for diversification before it is forced to appraise the declining profit position of the existing product line. Such opportunities may be created internally. For, as the firm operates for a long enough time, its managers and workers accumulate expertise or other specific assets from learning-by-doing. This may take many forms : a new product design or a change in technology may be discovered; the firm may develop marketing expertise and identify a related product into which expansion would be profitable; or they may simply develop a managerial talent which enables them to enter a related line of production. The emergence of opportunities to increase the profit of the firm provide the motivation for the diversification decision.

Managerial discretion in the product line choice can arise from several sources. In the early phases of the life cycle of any product the difference between sales revenue and variable costs (usually designated as contribution) is high and provides a relatively effortless way of generating profits for the firm if only the managers are willing to take the risks. The necessity for and the feasibility of maximizing profit from every one of the joint products, either individually or collectively, may also be diluted so long as an adequate number of profit generating opportunities are available either through the market itself or as a result of conscious managerial choices. Bates and Parkinson (1982, p.307) and Levy (1986) contend that the product line choice of the firm may also be justified on the ground that diversification, by spreading the risks over a variety of activities of the company may provide market stability and greater long run security.

A further remark, attributable to Penrose (1959), is important. So long as funds are available and they are not required to defend an existing market position, the incentives to invest in the growth of fixed assets and diversification manifest themselves. The management decides to forego short term profits in favor of long run objectives.

1.4. Organizational Structure

The other important aspect of largeness of size is the necessity to search for a more efficient organization. For, no one manager within the firm can have all the information and coordination capabilities. When the firm is specializing in a single product the obvious choice for the general manager (or, alternatively, the CEO, i.e., the chief executive officer) is to create functional divisions, delegate responsibility to the divisional managers, and make attempts to coordinate their activities. The U-form organizational structure came into being as a result of this imperative. Two issues are pertinent in such a context.

(a) The CEO is now subject to information asymmetry. Since it is expensive to retain information acquisition and control functions, which are essential to ensure profit maximization, there will be a tradeoff of profits to reduce the information overload.

(b) The divisional managers do not have sufficient information about how their activities can maximize profits. They may also pursue goals unrelated to profit maximization in the interest of divisional harmony. See, for instance, Marginson (1985).

This signals the possibility of extensive managerial discretion not acknowledged so far.

The cost reduction achieved in practice by adopting the M-form organizational structure and the consequent possibility of generating greater profit may itself be a source of discretionary managerial behavior[8]. For, such a division of labor implies that each of the organizational units have subgoals which can be at variance with the organizational objective. Cooperation and subgroup compliance can be achieved only if the organizational

---

8. Cable (1988, p.20) argued that " profit maximizing behavior at the top level remains only an assumption underlying the M-form hypothesis, and perhaps its strongest assumption. The desirable control properties of the M-form in constraining lower level behavior towards an overall objective, and avoiding organizational chaos after rapid and diversified expansion (cannot be taken for granted)."

objective is compromised while accommodating the aspirations of divisional managers and their autonomy. Knight (1933, p.22), Marshall et al (1984, p.9), DeAlessi and Staff (1987, pp.5 ff), Cable (1988), and Hill (1984) also indicated the possibility of moral hazard in the pursuit of divisional goals[9]. There are two aspects of this problem.

(a) Hexter (1975) pointed out that the management cannot distribute fixed costs and the internal transaction costs among the different products in any objective way. This makes it difficult to monitor the costs of each of the product divisions.

(b) As DeAlessi and Staff (1987, pp.5ff) indicated, a M-form organization and delegation of decision making can lead to shirking since the profit attributable to each of the product divisions cannot be measured seperately.

These features tend to impose significant monitoring and transaction costs due to the information impactedness and loss of control due to delegation of power even if the general manager insists on profit maximization. Managerial discretion manifests itself in a significant way.

1.5. Corporate Control

The large size of these firms implies that it is not possible for any one entrepreneur to finance the capital assets and accept the liabilities in case of a loss. As such there will be many owners (shareholders) who will finance the capital assets of the firm and accept the liability limited to their own share of investments in the firm. As Berle and Means (1932) noted, this gives rise to diffused shareholding, a tendency on the part of individual shareholders to free ride on the decisions of the others, and a seperation of the ownership from the management.

---

9. The following observation of Knight (1933,p.22) is noteworthy. "Organizations are like water-drops, or snow-balls, or any other large mass; the larger they are the more easily they are broken into pieces, the larger in proportion is the amount of energy that must be consumed in merely holding them together."

However, the shareholders (along with the other stakeholders, e.g., the term lending institutions) have the right to govern and make decisions. For, as Fama (1990, p.S 78) remarked, contracts in organizations usually contain the provision that the rights regarding the decisions that affect the net cashflows are largely in the realm of the equity holders because they bear the risks. Even so, due to lack of expertise and/or information asymmetry, the shareholders may find it more economical to delegate strategic decisions to the board of directors and the operational decisions to the managers. In general, almost all the managerial theories of the firm postulate that under these conditions the board of directors and/or the management may

(a) gain control over the decision making mechanisms of the firm, and

(b) not emphasize profit maximization as the predominant objective.

Instead, they may endeavor to maintain the operations of the firm at a level where they can minimize outside interference and preserve the autonomy of the managerial team. This has been argued cogently in Hill and Jones (1992, pp.134 ff). The large number of shareholders may find it expensive to control the discretionary behavior of the management.

The most important long term decision in such a context is the determination of the capital structure (more specifically the debt equity ratio). For, a large debt equity ratio is one of the major sources available to the management in their quest for corporate control. However, several consequences of this choice will have to be taken into consideration while arriving at this decision.

In the short run, the capital structure of the firm has a major influence on the firm's expected marginal cost of conducting its business during a given interval of time. In particular, as Vickers (1987, p.33 and 61) put it, "the higher the debt equity ratio, or the higher the degree of financial leverage at work in the firm, the greater will be the risk of exposure of both the creditors, that is the debt holders, and the residual owners." Hence, the firm will have to pay a higher rate of interest on its debt capital as the debt equity ratio increases. This reduces the short run profits of the firm. That is, an increase in the debt equity ratio, to the extent it raises the fixed cost of project financing, results in a financial risk. For, when the business risk is high and the returns from investment are uncertain the management cannot assure the shareholders that the anticipated profits will be realized at the expected time.

In the long run, an increase in the debt equity ratio entails a greater repayment committment from the
(a) profits of the firm during a specific interval of time,
(b) the reserves and surpluses of the firm, or
(c) from the market value of the capital assets of the firm in case of liquidation.
That is, in the long run, there is an increased risk of reduction in the market value of the common stock when the debt equity ratio increases. Smith and Watts (1992) argued that the managers should not be allowed to finance the investments in capital assets by increasing the debt equity ratios due to the potential for bankruptcy if there is any business risk at all.

On the positive side, as Grossman and Hart (1982, p.109) noted, by issuing debt the "management deliberately changes its incentives in such a way as to bring them into line with those of the shareholders because of the effect on market value. In other words, the management bonds itself to act in the shareholders' interest." Similarly, Easterbrook (1984) and Fama (1990, p.S89) pointed out that the managers may consider the issue of bonds as a way to convince the shareholders of their bonding by providing centralized monitoring of default risks by financial intermediaries, auditors, and others who specialize in evaluating such risks. That is, the debt equity ratio chosen by the management can be looked upon as a bonding device.

To what extent does the choice of the debt equity ratio
(a) affect the profits or the market value of the firm ?, and
(b) reflect the concern of the management to maximize profits, market value, or some other proximate objectives ?

At the present stage the literature cannot provide any conclusive answers to such questions.

1.6. Incentives and Monitoring

It is important to realize that the shareholders, or the board of directors acting on their behalf, can induce the management to bond with them by

(a) determining the compensation policies and the incentives offered to the management, and/or

(b) fixing the returns expected in the form of dividend payments.

However, it is not altogether clear that

(a) they are designed to maximize the market value of the firm, and

(b) the managerial responses will be adequate.

Most of the recent studies consider wage payments[10] to vary with the

(a) size represented by the level of sales,

---

10. In the early literature wage payments were considered as a managerial decision. Williamson's (1964, p.33) expense preference theory argued that managers tend to divert profits to perks. By expense preference Williamson means that " managers do not have a neutral attitude towards all classes of expenses. Instead, some types of expenses have positive values attached to them : they are incurred not merely for their contribution to productivity (if any), but, in addition, for the manner in which they enhance the individual and collective objectives of the managers." The reformulation of Edwards (1977) has influenced empirical work the most. However, as Mueller (1986, p.164) put it, "(a) large literature exists that attempts to explain managerial compensation. By and large, this literature has failed to develop hypotheses linking managerial compensation to managerial discretion, and has simply regressed various measures of compensation on sales and profits adjusting for the econometric problems inherent in this specification to varying degrees."

(b) strategies of the firm, and
(c) environmental considerations.
See, for instance, Flath and Knoeber (1985), Coughlan and Schmidt (1985), Skilvas (1987), and Garvey and Gaston (1991). However, it was pointed out that there can be situations in which the management would be willing to undertake value maximizing decisions only when the compensation they recieve is commensurate with the policies they have to pursue. Grabowski and Mueller (1972, p.9) and Smith and Watts (1992) found this hypothesis to be valid. Similarly, in some of the earlier literature, like McGuire et al (1962) it was pointed out that the wage payments are mostly related to past performance and cannot be interpreted as having any incentive effects[11].

There is no consensus of opinion regarding the reasons why shareholders offer stock ownership to the management. The following arguments are prevelant :
(a) When there is a high enough business risk the shareholders want to avoid a committment to the fixed wage payments. Instead they may make the management share the risk by offering a part of the common stock to them. See, for instance, Glazer and Israel (1990).
(b) Since the managers are generally risk averse they may not undertake even value increasing investments if there is any degree of business risk. One way to reduce agency costs and induce them to increase such investments is to offer them a stock ownership. See, for instance, Benston (1985), Murphy (1985), and Agrawal and Mandlekar (1987).

However, as managerial shareholding increases they gain control and tend to divert resources away from value maximization. An implication of this nature is evident in Santerre and Neun (1986), Williams (1987), Garvey and Gaston (1991), and Castanias and Helfat (1992). Hence, it is not always obvious that the

---

11. Drucker (1986,p.303) noted that compensation mechanisms can be notoriously ineffective. At best they can induce inefficient decision making if the payments are inadequate.

shareholders view the managerial shareholding as an incentive to bond with their objectives. Clearly, there is a limit on the shareholding of the management which the shareholders consider desirable.

On the other hand, consider the reasons for the management being motivated to hold a share of the common stock. The following arguments are pertinent :

(a) It provides them income in the form of dividends so long as they retain the stock and/or the market value of the firm if they sell it. Most of the earlier studies, like McGuire et al (1962), Mason (1971), and others treated it as such. The management may accept this as one source of income. But, as Williams (1987) pointed out, a small shareholding cannot make any material difference to the management in the context of income generation.

(b) It has been often recognized that receiving incentives in the form of shareholding restricts the managers from diversifying their portfolio sufficiently. See, for instance, Agrawal and Mandlekar (1987).

Hence, it can at best be concluded that managerial shareholding is one form of compensation though of dubious value to the management and its magnitude cannot be systematically explained by the shareholders' strategic considerations[12].

Studies relating to dividend decisions is rather extensive. In the early literature Lintner (1956) argued that the shareholders prefer to claim a steady rate of dividend when they find a significant business risk in order to avoid the prospect of not being able to recover adequate returns through long term capital gains. In general, as Walter (1963, p.280) and Vickers (1968,1987) argued, the net cashflow constrains the investment and dividend decisions. If, as Kort (1990, p.377) and DeAlessi and Fishe (1987, p.43) pointed out, there is an opportunistic behavior on the part of

---

12. Flath and Knober (1985) argued that other forms of compensation, such as a bonus payment for good performance, may serve the purpose just as well.

managers by increasing the investments in the firm there is a risk of the firm going bankrupt before the dividend payments materialize. The shareholders claim higher dividends as soon as possible to avoid such contingency. See Jorgensen et al (1989, p.339,365) and Rao and Sharma (1984).

How do managers respond to the constraint? As Grabowski and Mueller (1972, p.10) put it, "some dividends will probably be paid because they yield utility to the managers by increasing their security against a takeover." Similarly, as remarked in Walter (1963, p.287), Rozeff (1982, p.251), and succintly summarized in Copeland and Weston (1988, p.568), management, when they are making the dividend decision, may consider it as a bonding device. For, given the investments which they undertake, higher dividends assure the shareholders of the future prospects of the firm.

In general, it appears that incentives and monitoring do have the salutary effect of making the managers align their decisions with the interests of the shareholders. However, there is persuasive evidence to the argument of Garvey and Gaston (1991, p.105) that managers who enjoy some discretion rather than be under compulsion to serve the shareholder interest will be better inclined to fulfil implicit contracts.

1.7. Nature of the Study

It is evident from the foregoing presentation that the nature of the product markets and the seperation of ownership from control may enable the management of the firm to reduce profit or the market value of the firm in their quest to achieve other objectives if they are so inclined. A certain amount of control by the board of directors, as representatives of the shareholders and other major stakeholders, may place some effective restraints. However, the complexity of the organization and delegation of responsibility places two limits on the BOD :

(a) The BOD cannot have all the requisite information regarding the mechanisms through which a particular division contributes to the market value of the firm as well as its magnitude.

(b) The BOD may find it difficult to calibrate the extent of diversions and moral hazard in seperate divisions primarily due to information asymmetry and the costs involved in devising extensive control mechanisms.

The management, in its turn,

(a) is not in a position to calibrate its contribution to the market value of the firm since it may be far removed from it given the organizational hierarchy, and

(b) places a greater emphasis on harmony and cooperation within the division as a survival strategy.

Thus, as Hoenack (1983) and Rao (1989) emphasized, managerial discretion persists due to the organizational arrangements even if control mechanisms place some limits on it.

Earlier literature emphasized

(a) market imperfection, and

(b) seperation of ownership from control

as the sources of managerial discretion. The above argument indicates that they are necessary conditions but not sufficient for its existence. On the other hand, more recent studies indicate that the organizational structure provides sufficient leverage to the management to exercise their discretion[13].

The basic necessity is to examine the sources and extent of discretion at the different levels of the managerial hierachy. Hence, as Barney (1986, p.141, emphasis added) pointed out, "until organization- economic concepts are more fully developed to explain the behavior (within firms) they will be of less utility in organization theory (and business policy) than was pointed out." However, stated in such general terms, the task is too large and intractible. Hence, an attempt will be made to concentrate on a few major short run and long run managerial decisions.

---

13. The internal decision process may also contribute to the inelasticity of demand for the firm's products and reinforce on resouce diversions. However, this is likely to be a second order effect.

The analytical framework will however be developed in a rather general setting. Further extensions can therefore be developed depending on what the analyst wants to emphasize. Such efforts will be subject to limitations of available information.

1.8. Organization of the Study

A description of the possible organizational structures, patterns of delegation of authority, and the nature of managerial discretion will be outlined in chapter 2. Chapter 3 describes in detail the economic theory underlying the modelling structure of the present study. Chapter 4 considers the difficulties encountered by the existing studies in the specification of the model and its estimation and proposes a new method which can be shown to follow naturally from the underlying economic theory. Operational content can be provided only by defining the data base and the issues of measurement of relevant variables. This will be attempted in chapter 5. Chapter 6 considers the basic long run choices of the management. Chapters 7 and 8 deal with the short run decision making process. An overview of the results and future directions of research will be taken up in chapter 9.

CHAPTER 2

THE CORPORATE DECISION PROCESS

2.1. The Milieu

Almost all business opportunities are generated from two sources:
(a) the consumers visualize the need for a certain product or a service, express their willingness to pay for it, and the business units respond to the prospects of earning profits, and/or
(b) the entrepreneur conceptualizes the possibility of producing a certain product or service, convinces the potential consumer of its use, and earns a profit in the transaction.
To a large extent neither the market environment nor the distinctive competencies of the firm will, by themselves, be sufficient to create a successful product. For, following Whittington (1988, p.256) and Lyles and Schwenk (1992, pp.157-8), it can be argued that it is not easy to define the market environment the way it is. It can be realized only through the perceptions of the management which has been built up over time in the form of distinctive competencies. In general, the strategy of the firm depends upon the expectations regarding the market potential and the managerial perceptions of organizational capabilities.

Invariably every strategy of the firm can be implemented only through a proper organizational structure[1]. Two aspects should be kept in perspective :
(a) The design of the organizational structure depends on the requirements of decentralization, especially the optimality of information flows, (i.e., avoiding information asymmetry), and the degree to which deviations from optimality (moral hazard) will have to be controlled, and
(b) Extensive organizational changes are expensive to implement and

---

1. The contingency theorists emphasize the strategy-structure fit. See, for example, Hitt and Ireland (1986), Donaldson (1987), and Hamilton and Shergill (1992).

as such the competencies acquired by the management will also constrain the choices to some extent.
However, neither the organizational structure of the firm nor the distinctive competencies embodied therein can be taken to be invariant over time. Instead, there are at least two possibilities:
(a) managerial competencies may exhibit a degree of adaptivity and change depending upon the environmental realities, and
(b) at least to a certain extent managerial talent to organize production based on new strategies can be acquired from the market.

The corporate strategy and organizational structure are only indicative of the potential to generate profits. The essence of the operational details of the management is to translate these into reality. See, for instance, Learned et al (1969, pp.178 ff). To a large extent the implementation process necessitates an appropriate organizational control. Consequently, every organizational structure contains a specification of the
(a) information flows between the different echelons of the firm, and
(b) control mechanisms to reduce the moral hazard intrinsic to decentralized decision making within the firm.
However, it has been pointed out that such inbuilt procedures are inadequate to eliminate the moral hazard possibility. Instead, the CEO has to continuously monitor divisional performance to attenuate internal control loss and ensure that the expected performance materializes. In general, as Rao and Saha (1994 a) reported
(a) the success of an organizational strategy depends upon appropriate monitoring and control of the implementation of managerial strategy, and
(b) short run market fluctuations will necessitate some fine tuning with respect to control.

Managerial discretion can occur in any of these stages. In particular,
(a) in the formulation of the strategy the management may stop short of the optimum product diversity or undertake an excessive

amount of it,
(b) the management may not choose an appropriate organizational structure, and/or
(c) there may be inefficiency at the level of operational execution.
Each of these aspects has implications for the short run profit generation as well as the market value of the firm.

Consequently, an identification of the sources of managerial discretion necessitates the examination of the interrelationships between
(a) the strategies of the firm,
(b) the choice of the organizational structure,
(c) the control mechanisms in the implementation process, and
(d) the implications of these choices for the performance of the firm.

2.2. The U-Form Organization

It was noted in section 1.4 that the large size of the firm and the information overload necessitates decentralization in the form of a U-form organizational structure. A single product or a group of related products will generally make such an organizational structure conducive to developing distinctive competencies in functional areas.

A broad understanding of the decision making process can be obtained by considering
(a) the long term or strategic decisions, and
(b) the operating decisions
seperately. In general, the significant long term decisions are
(a) choice of the product range or the diversification decision,
(b) acquisition of the physical capital assets, and
(c) long term financial decisions (capital structure).
In the short run, the management has to operate the assets of the firm. The basic decisions relate to
(a) monitoring the market environment, choice of production levels of the various products, and the choice of advertising policies

and other marketing strategies,
(b) organizing production by choosing appropriate workforce, incentives, and inventory policies,
(c) identifying adequate sources of working capital to ensure that the operations of the firm can be carried out as planned, and
(d) the distribution of gains among the stakeholders; in particular, the choice of the dividends per share.

The diffused shareholding, which results in the information asymmetry and lack of a coherent group of shareholders who have the expertise to manage the firm, necessitate delegation of decision making to the management. The common arrangement is an implicit contract between the board of directors and the management. The understanding would be that the managers are delegated the powers of decision making with respect to their decisions because they have superior information and they can be expected to act in the interests of the shareholders.

However, the information and the expertise needed to make the long term decisions is generally different from the requirements of the short run decisions. Hence, these decisions will be delegated to different teams of managers. In addition, the board may want to maintain supervision over the long term strategies while delegating the short run operational responsibilities to the CEO[2]. Fig.2.1 is a representation of such an arrangement.

---

2. As Chandler (1990, pp.424-5) noted, this is a legal requirement for the AG companies in Germany. They are required to have
(a) a supervisory board which is responsible for control and guidance with respect to long term planning, and
(b) a management board which is responsible for the running of routine business.
In contrast, the privately held limited liability company GmbH has no such legal requirement. However, in practice they also find the two board system efficient. In almost all other countries the same organizational arrangements appear to persist though the legal framework will differ somewhat.

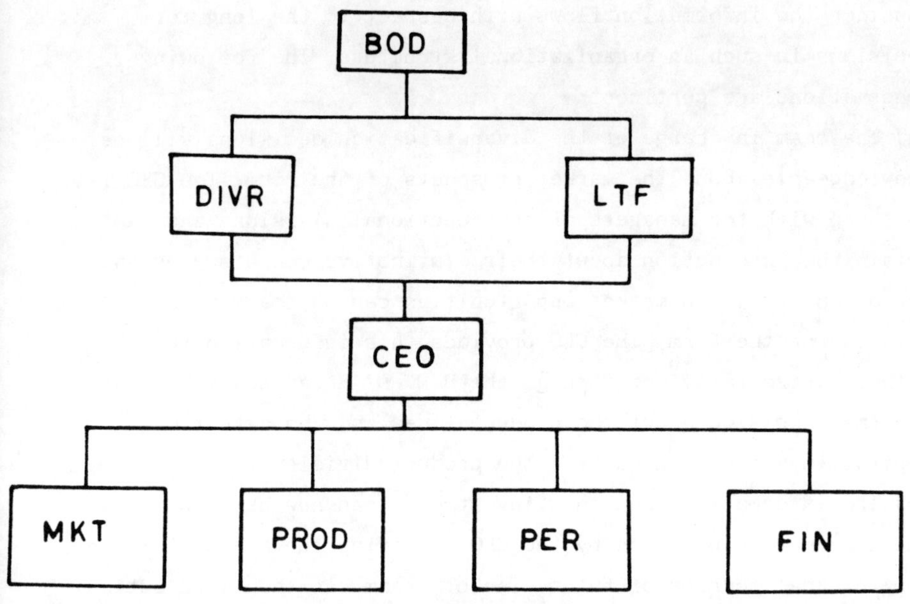

FIG. 2.1. DECENTRALIZED ORGANIZATION

LEGEND

BOD - Board of Directors

DIVR - Product Diversification Decision

LTF - Long Term Financing

CEO - Chief Executive Officer

MKT - Marketing Manager

PROD - Production Manager

PER - Personnel Manager

FIN - Financial Manager

Consider the information flows with respect to the long term decisions in such an organizational structure. The following observations are pertinent:

(a) The team in charge of the diversification decisions will be knowledgeable about the market prospects of the firm. The CEO is in touch with the managers of the functional divisions and can obtain the information about their distinctive competencies and the extent to which market opportunities can be translated into profits for the firm. The CEO provides this information to DIVR either horizontally[3] or through the BOD. DIVR can now make a well informed decision about the product lines and the extent of capital investment in each of the product divisions.

(b) The information about new investments can now be combined with the information provided by the CEO regarding the availability of the internal sources of funds. The LTF team can then work out an optimal financial mix.

Can these management teams at the different divisional levels have any discretion in this set up? Clearly, each of the teams has the autonomy to process and interpret the information they recieve. Each of them also feel that they have their own prestige to defend. In particular, note the following aspects.

(a) If the DIVR team recommends very little diversification capital resources will remain underutilized and/or the market share will remain low. On the other hand, if they encourage excessive diversification the market value of the firm cannot be maximized.

They will choose some balance between these two aspects.

(b) The LTF team cannot recommend too low a volume of finances or

---

3. Most recent studies emphasize the advantages of horizontal communication over vertical or hierarchical communication when there is a time lag and/or loss of information. See, for instance, Welch (1980), Bartlett and Ghosal (1987), and Wanvani (1993). In general, the concept of quality circles in the Japanese management practice is a good approximation to the idea of horizontal communication.

a low debt equity ratio since this can result in a paucity of funds. Too large a debt equity ratio entails an excessive interest burden. Their choice will depend on how they evaluate these two opposing forces.

In general, it can be claimed that the long term decisions may still indicate trading off market value of the firm to
(a) achieve a larger market share dynamically,
(b) have the potential to prempt competition, and
(c) maintain a comfortable financial base.

Turning to the operating decisions under CEO coordination the following information advantages of delegated decisions should be recorded[4]
(a) The marketing manager has the best information about
(i) the existing markets and their dynamics,
(ii) the emerging markets, and
(iii) the potential to develop markets by appropriate promotion strategies.
The CEO therefore expects from the marketing manager decisions regarding
(i) sales targets for the various products of the firm, and
(ii) the selling expenses which will be necessary to maintain the desired position.
(b) The production manager will then be expected to
(i) schedule production operations, and
(ii) define the inventory policies in such a way that the selling strategies of the marketing manager can be fulfilled.

---

4. It is fairly clear that the relationship between the BOD and the CEO is an implicit contract. It is possible that the preferences of these two groups are also at variance. The general feeling is that the moral hazard problem increases the further away a manager is from the BOD in an organizational hierarchy. However, the information available is almost never adequate to conceptualize analysis at this level.

(c) The personnel manager has an important supporting role. The choice of

(i) an adequate amount of workforce, as well as

(ii) the incentives and control exercised in fulfilling production targets will ultimately determine the success of the firm.

(d) The production scheduling will be made known to the financial manager. Value increasing prospects of the firm may be jeopardized if

(i) there is too little working capital, or

(ii) expensive financial sources remain unutilized.

Clearly, the coordination and control functions are vested in the CEO.

It is evident that there will be pervasive managerial discretion in these decision processes[5]. Since these aspects will be considered in detail in subsequent chapters only one aspect will be highlighted here.

Consider the decision making process of the financial manager. The proximate objectives are[6]

(a) to ensure that production is not reduced due to shortage of working capital, and

(b) to keep the interest burden of conducting a given volume of sales as low as possible.

---

5. It has not been possible so far to provide an operational procedure for estimating the costs due to information asymmetry and/or moral hazard. Only a few theoretical attempts by Hoenack (1983), and Leibenstein (1980) are available.

6. It is important to realize that the financial manager cannot know the contribution of his decisions to the market value of the firm. Hence, even the CEO cannot advise the financial manager to maximize the market value of the firm. Proximate objectives being attributed to different functional divisions is the rule rather than the exception.

Consider the ratio of interest payments to the cost of goods sold (denoted as FIRI). If the amount of working capital available to the firm is low the interest burden is low but the loss of production is disproportionately larger. FIRI tends to be high. As the volume of working capital increases and facilitates planned levels of production FIRI decreases. However, beyond a threshold limit the idle funds increase the costs without contributing to production and/or sale. FIRI rises again. In general, referring to Fig. 2.2, FIRI has a U-shape when plotted against working capital

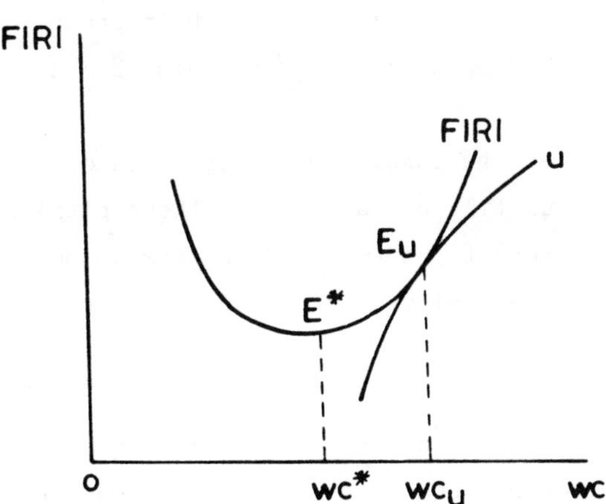

FIG. 2.2. WORKING CAPITAL CHOICE

(WC). The financial manager will generally assign

(a) a negative value to FIRI, and

(b) a positive value to WC so that value increasing prospects may not be jeopardized.

That is, the preferences of the managers will be of the form

$U = - FIRI + \lambda WC ; \lambda > 0.$

Hence, the actual choice $WC_u > WC^*$. This manifestation of managerial discretion is a distinct possibility.

Notice that the control aspects specified so far are only those built into the organizational chart. As remarked earlier, these would be inadequate to reduce managerial discretion. Usually the following additional controls are utilized as and when applicable and efficacious:

(a) physical or quantitative targets to each division,

(b) budgeting and auditing,

(c) constraints in the form of dividend payments, and

(d) incentives like wages, perks, and stock options.

Hoenack (1983) and Burton and Obel (1984) made attempts to examine the optimum combination of controls in different settings. However, as of now, it is unrealistic to argue that closed ended solutions are available.

2.3. The M-Form Organization

It is well known that many firms diversified their production into both related and unrelated products. The following broad generalization is possible :

(a) Suppose the synergies are purely technological and can be exploited by using the unutilized capacity of the capital assets of the firm. If the different products of the firm do not require any specific skills and centralized coordination of production is efficient the U-form organization is adequate.

(b) However, the markets for these products may be geographically dispersed. If different marketing information is necessitated and/or different strategies need to be conceptualized for each market delegation of responsibility based on information advantages will be efficient[7]. An M-form organizational structure emerges.

(c) Let the synergies emerge from the marketing expertise or R & D

---

7. One further informational advantage of the M-form has been noted. Marginson (1985, p.41), Kinnie (1987, pp.467 ff), and Colling and Ferner (1992, p.216) considered the example of strong labor unions. When confronted by them, divisionalization helps in keeping

(a) problems and conflicts isolated to the divisional level, and

(b) bargaining at the divisional level distinct.

On the other hand, a global solution, initiated by the headquarters, as in the U-form, will spread the problems to the other divisions as well.

activities. For example, the wide network of marketing personnel built up by Brooke Bond could also identify the potential to enter into related and/or unrelated food products. Though the marketing resource is common the technology of unrelated products may necessitate different types of expertise. Once again reorganizing the firm along M-form lines is effective[8].

Fundamentally the M-form organization emphasizes the advantages of decentralization. As Williamson (1964, p.134) put it, the "organization and operation of the large scale enterprise along the lines of the M-form favors goal pursuit and least cost behavior more nearly associated with the neoclassical profit maximization hypothesis than does the U-form alternative". However, decentralization does not necessarily confirm autonomy to the divisional managers. For, as noted in Williamson (1986, p.180), "some divisionalized companies are essentially holding companies, in that they lack the requisite control machinery, while others are nominally divisionalized, with the general office maintaining extensive involvement in operating affairs." Hence, as Hill (1984, p.55) noted, it is essential to provide decentralized decision-making responsibilities to divisional managers if the firm has to achieve beneficial motivational effects, and encourage initiative and responsibility at the divisional level. Further, it

---

8. As Kay (1984) and Barney and Ouchi (1986, pp.158 ff) noted, when there is complete independence between the products of the firm the distinction between the M-form and the H-form (the holding company) will not be substantial. For, the only difference is in the ownership of divisions and the problems associated with ownership and control. M-form structures would be far more important in cases where the products are somewhat related either technologically or through the market. Hence, one of the principles of M-form organizations is to define product divisions in such a way that the interactions between divisions are eliminated and those within divisions are maximized. A rather succint statement of this issue can be found in Tirole (1988, pp.48 ff) and Holstrom and Tirole (1989, p.126).

should be noted that the existence of common resources and the synergies implied in their use is an equally important dimension pointing to the need for coordination among autonomous divisions. For, the high profitability of a particular product division at a point of time may not ensure its continuation dynamically. The managers at the divisional level cannot judge the fluctuations in market conditions since they are
(i) engrossed in the day to day operating details, and
(ii) further removed from the source of this information.
Hence, capital allocation and financial committments on this account cannot be left to the individual divisions. This strategic decision is consequently centralized in the hands of the specialized staff at the headquarters. Williamson (1986, p.179 ff) and Varadarajan and Ramanujam (1990, p.475) emphasized this aspect. As the latter pointed out, "pursuing a philosophy of decentralization may be necessary in response to the relatively high level of product line breadth and geographic diversification in many firms. The concommitant use of tight financial control and reporting systems appear to be indicative of a conscious effort by these firms to manage the structural complexity entailed by a strategy of product and market diversification." In otherwords, the effectiveness of the M-form organizational structure of the firm depends crucially on the control which is provided in the implementation of the firm's strategy. See Rao and Saha (1994 a,b).

For all practical purposes Fig. 2.3 represents the organizational structure of the M-form enterprise. Four aspects should be kept in perspective:
(a) The long term strategic decision process will be very similar to the U-form. The DIVR and STAFF may both provide inputs regarding the market prospects of different products.
(b) The control function of STAFF is crucial though this adds a dimension of managerial discretion.
(c) The role of STAFF in relation to DIVR, LTF and BOD is always an implicit contract.
(d) Each of the product divisions may in turn operate as U-forms

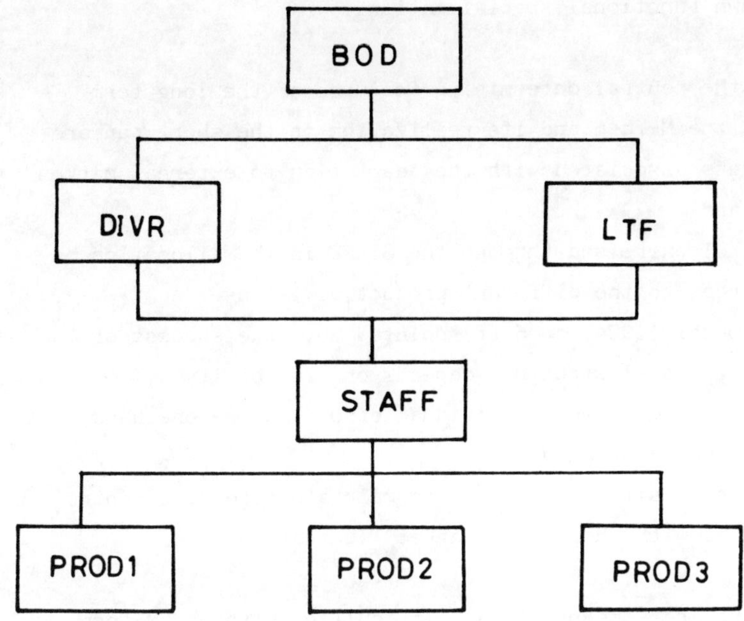

FIG. 2.3. THE M-FORM ORGANIZATION

LEGEND

STAFF - Specialists who allocate common resources

PROD 1,2,3 - Different Product Divisions

with their own functional specialization.

In general, the central determining features of the long term potential of the M-form and its realization in the short run are
(a) the success associated with the adaptation to external market conditions, and
(b) the control exercised through the STAFF in the allocation of common resources to the different product divisions.
That is, as Ouchi (1984, pp.6 ff) pointed out, the success of the M-form organizational structure depends on its ability to
(a) forge a balance between individual effort on the one hand, and team work on the other, and
(b) make the requisite adaptations to maintain effective control when confronted with short term market fluctuations.

However, there are some practical difficulties with the M-form conceptualization which signal managerial discretion.
(a) Delegation of functional activities to each of the different product divisions may be inefficient. There are two aspects of this problem :
(i) As Dow (1988) pointed out, it may be far more economical for the headquarters to procure some common inputs instead of allowing each of the divisions to do their purchasing independently. For, they may be able to obtain larger discounts and reduce transportation and/or inventory costs due to the bulk purchase.
(ii) Hill (1988, pp.80 ff) pointed out that different products of the firm, even if they are technologically unrelated, may be marketed in a package or through the same marketing and sales personnel.
(b) Informational difficulties arise when there are fluctuating markets. Both the collection and dissemination of information from and to various levels of hierarchy becomes extensive and time consuming as the size of the organization increases. M-form firms tend to falter whenever there is an urgency for making appropriate strategic decisions and/or a necessity for obtaining the missing information for making an efficient choice. See Bolton and Farrell (1990).
(c) There is a possibility of inadequate information to make an

optimal allocation of resources. For, as Hexter (1975) and DeAlessi and Staff (1987, pp.5 ff) pointed out, the staff attached to the BOD cannot distribute the fixed costs and the internal transaction costs among the different products in any objective way. This makes it difficult to ascertain the profit attributable to each of the product divisions and/or monitor the costs. The information impactedness and loss of control due to delegation of power results in the discretionary use of resources even if the general manager insists on profit maximization.

(d) There is always a possibility of moral hazard. This can take several forms:

(i) Some problems are inherent in the emphasis on short term profit maximization. For example, Hill (1988, p.80) noted that in an attempt to meet the head office determined profit goals divisional managers may cut expenditures on R & D, market research and so on which they judge to be non-essential in the short run. This results in a decline in the market value of the firm in the long run.

(ii) Over time the members of a subdivision come to know each other rather well and generate mutually self-serving objectives. Such an understanding may reduce the productivity of the workers and reduce the overall efficiency of the enterprise. See, for example, Wintrobe and Breton (1986,pp.532 ff). Stated more generally, division of labor of the M-form nature implies that each of the organizational components may have subgoals which are at variance with the organizational objectives of profit maximization.

(iii) As Hoenack (1983, p.37) noted, the managers of each of the product divisions of the M-form know their contribution (difference between sales revenue and variable costs) to the profit of the enterprise. They will therefore ask for a share of it if cooperation is expected from them. They will have no incentive to maintain efficiency and comply with the profit maximization objective of the BOD if they do not get the share of profits which they consider equitable. Also see Gaynor (1989, p.59).

(iv) Marginson (1985) as well as FitzRoy and Kraft (1987) noted that the equity issues may strain the relationship between the divisions and the central office to a point where unionization emerges. This reduces the ability of the M-form structure to maximize profits.

In general, as Phillips (1962, pp.27 ff) and Hill and Pickering (1986, p.170) argued,
(a) managers of product divisions may have their own localized objectives,
(b) the reneging cannot be fully controlled by the central office due to the information impactedness which they experience, and
(c) cooperation and subgroup compliance can be achieved only if the organizational objective of profit maximization is compromised while accommodating the aspirations of the divisional managers and their autonomy.

Despite the fact that these possibilities arise their actual quantitative impact is unknown. Williamson (1971, pp. 377 ff), in particular, argued that such inefficiencies will only be a one time exception. For, the lower level managers cannot repeatedly distort the information or disobey executive directives without attracting the attention of the specialized staff at the central office.

Williamson (1971, p.379) and Cable (1988, p.20) also acknowledged the possibility that the central office may itself consider company wide objectives, other than profit maximization, to be essential in the context of imperfect markets. Chief among them are
(a) maintaining market shares,
(b) growth of the capital assets of the firm, and
(c) corporate prestige in relation to their customers and shareholders.
On occasions, they may even make attempts to rescue a loss making division rather than divest from it.

2.4. The Major Lessons

In general, most of the large firms implement strategies by

utilizing a complex organizational structure. The U-form and the M-form are two such examples. Far more intricate coordination in the form of matrix organizations, team formation and so on has emerged. The central feature of all these organizational forms is decentralization and delegation of responsibility.

It is clearly understood that both information asymmetry and moral hazard are intrinsic to such organizational arrangements. Monitoring and control are expensive and information impactedness persists. An optimal balance between information acquisition and designing control mechanisms as against the efficiency gains of delegation of power is subjective and very dynamic.

In particular, it should be acknowledged that the divisional managers, especially in a functionally specialized enterprise, do not know how their actions contribute to the overall profit of the firm. The delegation of responsibility should specify the proximate objectives that they are expected to pursue. It is the role of the CEO or the STAFF in a M-form to see how best they can be defined to achieve the overall objectives of the enterprise.

2.5. Proximate Divisional Objectives

To begin with assume that the board of directors is inclined to maximize the market value of the firm. Then, given the information regarding the competencies of the management, the manager in charge of planning diversification can be expected to choose products which have the best potential to generate value. This will, in fact, be the goal specified for that division. However, risk averse management may feel that they should err on the conservative side and recommend less than the maximum that can be achieved. On the other hand, if the management attaches prestige to the size of the enterprise they may suggest a larger range of products at the expense of market value maximization.

The DIVR team will be under pressure to acquire physical assets necessary to implement the diversification program. Normally it can be expected that the LTF team will do it at the least possible cost consistent with value maximization. However, cost increases are likely if the acquisition of assets over a short time horizon is emphasized.

Consider the team arranging the long term finances. Clearly they will be expected to choose a financial mix, in particular the debt equity ratio, in such a way as to minimize the cost of financing in an effort to maximize the value of the firm. However, it is evident from the descriptions of chapter 1, that they may place a value on the control dimension.

In sum, the divisional managers in charge of long term planning and BOD are likely to specify maximization of the value of the firm as the major objective for long term decisions. The possibility that they will associate some positive value to market share and stability of operations cannot be ruled out apriori.

Turning to the operational decisions note that the marketing manager is likely to have the best information about the demand for the various products of the firm. Assume that the management is appraised of the cost structure in the production of various goods. The manager at this level can therefore be instructed to maximize short run profits by specifying the feasible volume of production of each product and back it up by appropriate promotion policies and selling costs. Since most of the firms in the corporate sector follow the retail price maintenance policy the proximate decisions of the management of this division are net sales and selling costs. The proximate objective is to maximize profits which alone will be in consonance with value maximization.

Consider the production manager. Given the choice of the various products the major goal of the management would be to choose the necessary personnel, provide the necessary incentives in the form of wages, and motivate them to maximize sales. In general, when the markets for different products are fluctuating and uncertain, it may not be economical to vary production significantly from one period to the next. To reduce the costs dynamically the management may supplement its production plans with an inventory policy.

Short term financial management consists of arranging the necessary working capital at the lowest possible costs. The appropriate financial mix is the obvious decision for this division.

The basic point that emerges from this analysis is that proximate objectives can be conceptualized for each division and implemented in such a way that the overall goal of value maximization can be pursued. This will be the realistic standpoint from which the rest of the analysis of decentralized organizational decision making can proceed.

2.6. Need for Progress

Empirical information on the nature and extent of tradeoffs between different objectives is however nonexistent. Hence, as Kay (1991, p.62) pointed out, "the key role for the development of microeconomics in the next century is whether (the organizational arrangements of the firm) can be expressed and developed in ways which give them relevance to business policy."

Such developments have already been initiated. For, as Porter (1981, p.610) noted, "exposure to business policy concepts is having a decidedly positive influence on organizational research ...". Despite the evidence of convergence the progress over the past decade has been rather fragmentary. Progress will be slow unless painstaking efforts, at both the theoretical and empirical levels, are forthcoming.

The rest of the present study is an attempt to initiate research in this interface between organizational economics and business policy.

CHAPTER 3

MODELLING FRAMEWORK

3.1. The Issues

The description of the decentralized decision making process in chapter 2 indicates that the managers at each of the hierarchical levels

(a) will generally be aware of the proximate objectives of the higher level controllers,

(b) know that the higher level controllers can calibrate the effect of managerial decisions on the attainment of their objectives,

(c) will take into account the incentives provided and the control being exercised on their decisions, and

(d) have preferences and priorities which are specific to their division.

The choices of the management take this information into account.

Consider the managerial team in charge of the diversification decision. Clearly, the choices regarding product lines have implications for the long run performance of the firm. Hence, the board of directors, as representatives of the shareholders, will be concerned with the effect of product diversification on the market value of the capital assets of the firm. In particular, they may reveal to the management that their objective is to maximize the market value of the firm.

To understand the nature of the relationship between the diversification decision and market value consider the following. When the firm is specializing in the production of its primary product it can be expected that

(i) many profitable opportunities exist, and

(ii) there are unutilized capital resources and distinctive competencies within the firm so that there will be a positive organizational response to the introduction of new products.

Hence, an increase in the market value can be achieved by

diversification. However, when the product range crosses a threshold there are adverse effects on the market value of the firm. The three basic reasons are

(i) there are lower rates of profit on the investments in the new products being introduced because the market opportunities are subject to diminishing returns,

(ii) the new products may displace old products (cannibalize their market demand) rather than create new markets (especially when they are related or substitutable), and

(iii) there are limits on the distinctive competencies of the firm (including its capacity to attract appropriate managerial talent from the market).

Hence, in general, the market value of the firm has an inverted U-shape with respect to the degree of diversification. This is represented in Fig. 3.1. The managerial team must consider this as a constraint on their decision making.

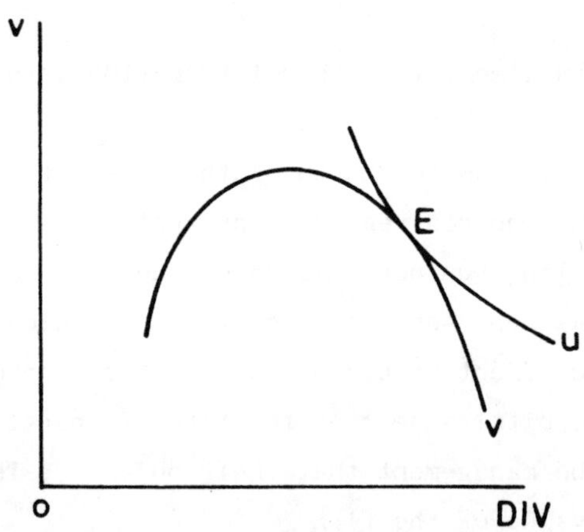

FIG. 3.1. THE DIVERSIFICATION DECISION

However, greater diversification, when implemented through a divisionalized organizational structure, provides them greater prestige and power. It may also have a salutary effect on the stability of the market share of the firm. The managerial team is likely to place a positive value on these objectives while keeping the market value constraint in perspective. This is represented as the U-curve in Fig. 3.1. The indifference curve in the (V,D) plane is negatively sloped.

The board of directors, in their turn, realize these possibilities of resource diversions. To curb these tendencies they offer incentives to ensure compliance or device monitoring mechanisms to restrict the management. The diversification decision will be subject to these constraints as well.

In the short run the marketing manager is monitoring the product market fluctuations and recommends an appropriate amount of sales for each of the product lines of the firm. Some sales promotion strategies will be devised to defend their market position and/or aggresively make an attempt to improve their market share in certain product lines. The vice president, who is in charge of the short run utilization of the fixed assets of the firm, would surely be conscious of the contribution to profits of this particular division. This is a constraint on the decisions of the marketing manager.

In addition, the marketing manager realizes two other aspects.
(i) Targetting a very low volume of sales will not be in consonance with the profit goals. However, they may not be able to defend too high a target when subjected to market uncertainty.
(ii) An excessive selling expenditure may enable them to more readily defend a sales target that they set.
In other words, the survival instincts of the managerial team induces them to tradeoff profits to achieve other goals.

Consider the decisions of the production manager. The basic purpose of this division is to manage production and supply of different products in confirmity with the sales target. Two instruments are available to achieve this target.
(i) incentives for the workforce to adjust to production requirements if such a flexibility exists, and/or
(ii) hold appropriate inventories while maintaining a constant level of production.
Clearly, the perceptions of the production manager can be at

variance with cost minimization in their efforts to fulfil the sales targets.

In general, a generic specification of the modelling framework entails three aspects:
(a) specification of the choice set,
(b) constraints placed on the management by the higher level controller, and
(c) preferences of the divisional management.

One other issue should be kept in perspective while appraising the appropriateness of the model specification. The revealed preference argument can be invoked to understand the actual, or ex post, choices of the management. In particular, the management may choose a particular level of any specific decision variable for one of two reasons:
(a) they prefer it, or
(b) they are constrained to choose it.

To begin with note that the distinctive competencies of the management are fixed and limited at any given point of time even if they are variable dynamically. That is, larger values of the decision choices of the management are subject to diminishing returns. Hence, the relationship between the objectives of a higher level controller and the decisions of the management at a given level is generally of the inverted u-shape.

Three patterns of ex post choices can then be identified. Firstly, assume that
(a) there are unlimited market opportunities so that the extent to which the objective of a specific level of management within the firm can be achieved is only a function of the managerial choices,
(b) the management can easily satisfy the constraints placed on them by the higher level controller, and
(c) the management has a positive preference for the decisions they make, i.e., they are willing to tradeoff value to attain a higher level of the decision variable.
Under these circumstances the ex post choices of the management

would be governed exclusively by their preferences and would be independent of the
(a) market opportunities, and
(b) constraints placed on them.
Secondly, consider the possibility that
(a) there are limits on market opportunities,
(b) the constraints placed on the management are not binding, and
(c) the management is inclined to maximize the objective specified by the higher level of management.
In such a case, the choice of managerial decisions and the maximum attainable level of the specified goal are strictly functions of the market opportunities. They cannot be independent of these variables[1]. Thirdly, postulate that
(a) the market opprtunities are unlimited,
(b) the management has a positive preference for the decisions they make, and
(c) the constraints placed on the management are sufficiently severe so that they cannot be neglected in the interest of the survival of the management team.
Obviously, the management would modify their preferences and the ex post decision choices will depend on these constraints.

In general, the ex post decision choice has three components:
(a) a constant term which exclusively reflects managerial preferences,
(b) the effect of market opportunities and adjustments thereof, and
(c) the modifications brought about by the incentives offered and the constraints placed on the management by the controller.
The model specification must reflect these aspects of the decision making process.

---

1. Suppose there are managerial preferences for the decisions made. Then the ex post decisions will depend on market opportunities in addition to the fixed effect of the limited distinctive competencies.

In particular, a generic specification of the modelling framework entails three aspects:

(a) specification of the choice set,

(b) constraints placed by the higher level management, and

(c) preferences of the divisional manager.

Section 3.2 will be devoted to the details of the inadequacy of the existing specifications. A more reliable and theoretically defensible specification will be attempted in section 3.3. Section 3.4 examines some further practical difficulties which must be kept in perspective in the empirical analysis.

3.2. The Current Practice

Let G denote any general goal of the higher level manager. Usually this will be affected by the environmental conditions external to the division and the choices of the management under consideration. Let C denote the choice or decision of the management and X denote a market related variable or a characteristic representing the distinctive competencies of the division. Then, the valuation constraint (usually labelled as the valuation frontier) can be represented by

$G = G(C,X)$

Most of the studies assume that the valuation frontier can be approximated by

$$G = a_0 + a_1C + a_2C^2 + a_3X \ ; \ a_1 > 0, \ a_2 < 0$$

The usual justification, as noted in section 3.1, is that the relationship between G and C is of the inverted u-shape.

Assume, for the present, that the management chooses C so as to maximize G. The optimal choice of C is given by the equation

$$a_1 + 2a_2C = 0, \text{ or}$$

$$C = - (a_1/2a_2)$$

which is a constant independent of X. As noted in the previous

section this specification is inadequate for two reasons.
(a) This constant or fixed choice of C is not a result of the managerial preferences for C, and
(b) not being a function of X it fails to explain the observed variations in C over time.
This can also be viewed from a different perspective. Consider a unit change in C. Rewriting

$$G = a_0 + (a_1 + a_2C)C + a_3X$$

it follows that, starting from any level of C, a unit change in C contributes an amount $a_1 + a_2C$ to G on an average. This specification assumes that G is independent of the market conditions and/or the distinctive competencies of the management. This is theoretically indefensible. The term a_1C must be dropped from the specification.

However, notice that this is not a complete solution to the problem since the specification cannot sustain the inverted u-shape of the valuation frontier any longer.

Similarly, the managerial preference function is usually written as

$$U = G + \lambda_1C + \lambda_2Y \; ; \; \lambda_1 > 0$$

where Y is any variable which the management values either because it is an incentive or a constraint placed on them. The specification of $\lambda_1 > 0$ indicates the managerial preference to tradeoff G to attain a higher value of C.

Given this specification it follows that the value of C which maximizes U is given by

$$2a_2C + \lambda_1 = 0$$

The problem of the optimal C being independent of X and Y persists.

In general, the specification would be far more realistic if

$C = C(X,Y)$

indicating that the decisions of the management would be sensitive to variations in the market conditions as well as the constraints placed on them. The constant term in this equation, if any, would be a reflection of the managerial preferences alone. Such a specification is not available in the literature so far.

3.3. The Correct Formulation

Reconsider a change in any market related variable X. There are three possible perceptions of the management.

(a) The change in X is of a long term nature and it is possible to make changes in C without any additional cost. In such a case the entire change in X will be absorbed by a suitable choice of C without any additional cost.

(b) Only a part of the change in X is expected to be permanent or alternatively, a drastic change in C is considered expensive. If, however, some changes in C can be effected without any significant cost the management may consider it more prudent to adjust C at least partially.

(c) In some cases the change in X may be considered to be purely temporary. It may also be very expensive and impractical to make any changes in C in the short run.

In general, it would be realistic to expect that

$C = b_1X$

without any constant term in the specification. The magnitude of b_1 depends on the managerial perceptions alluded to above.

How does the valuation frontier change when X varies? An appropriate answer can be obtained in the following manner:

(a) if C adjusts fully to X, X will have no further effect on G. A unit change in C will then alter G by an amount a_1C on an average.

(b) Suppose C adjusts only partially. To that extent X would still have some effect on G. That is, the average contribution of a unit change in C to the variation in G can be written as

$$a_1^* = a_1C + a_2X$$

(c) X will have an autonomous effect on G (though not through C) when the management does not or cannot adjust C to the variation in X.

It should be reiterated that the choice of C can never be independent of the nature and extent of X. Hence, in general, the effect of a unit change in C on the valuation can be represented as

$$a_1^* = a_1C + a_2X$$

$$G = a_0 + a_1^*C + a_3Z$$

$$= a_0 + a_1C^2 + a_2CX + a_3Z$$

where the X variable is reclassified as a Z if the management considers it very expensive to accommodate in their decision making process. Clearly, a_2 and/or a_3 may be zero in practice. The introduction of the interaction term CX is the crucial change in the specification.

Notice that this specification accommodates both the properties alluded to in the previous section. In particular,

(a) since $a_1 < 0$ in general, the inverted u-shape of the valuation frontier is restored if $a_2 > 0$. For, G reaches a maximum at

$C = -(a_2/2a_1)X > 0$, and

(b) there is no constant term in the choice of C which maximizes G.

C is, in general, a function of X alone. Further, a unit change in X has an independent effect on G only when

(a) C adjusts only partially, or

(b) C cannot be adjusted to the variations in X.

The other important aspect is the specification of the managerial preference function. In particular, it should

(a) represent the possibility that the management places value on C independent[2] of Y, and

(b) exhibit the channels through which the variations in Y affect C.

The minimal specification of the preference function would be

$$U = G + \lambda_1^* C \; ; \; \lambda_1^* > 0$$

However, the utility or prestige which the management associates with a unit increase in C will be conditioned by

(a) the incentives provided (thus indicating their willingness to bond with the organizational goals), and/or

(b) the constraints placed on them (in order to ensure the stability of the team against takeover threats) by the higher level controller.

Hence, in general,

$$\lambda_1^* = \lambda_1 + \lambda_2 Y$$

$$U = G + \lambda_1^* C$$

$$= G + \lambda_1 C + \lambda_2 CY$$

provides a more appropriate specification of the managerial preferences. Fundamentally, this specification postulates that the changes in Y restrain the management in their urge to tradeoff G to pursue other objectives of their own interest. In its turn this will have implications for the choice of C by the management.

Suppose the management maximizes U, subject to the valuation constraint, in its choice of C. Then, the optimal choice of C is given by

---

2. The management places a value on X only in so far as it has an effect on the valuation frontier. Hence, they adjust C accordingly. There cannot be any further independent valuation which the management associates with X.

$$2a_1C + a_2X + \lambda_1 + \lambda_2Y = 0$$

so that

$$C = b_0 + b_1X + b_2Y$$

where $b_0 = -(\lambda_1/2a_1)$, $b_1 = -(a_2/2a_1)$, and $b_2 = -(\lambda_2/2a_1)$.

In general, a constant term can appear in this equation only through the managerial preference function.

It is clear from the above specification that
(a) there can be many independent decisions made by the management at each level of hierarchy, and
(b) X and Y can also be vector valued.
The most general form of the model will therefore be

Maximize $U = G + C'\lambda Y$
subject to

$$G = A_0 + C'A_1C + C'A_2X + A_3Z$$

where
C is a (px1) vector of managerial decisions,
X is a (qx1) vector of market related variables which affect the value recovered by the higher level controller,
Z is a (sx1) vector of variables which the management cannot, or does not, accommodate in their decision making process,
Y is a (rx1) vector of variables which the management values,
C' is the transpose of C, and
A_0, A_1, A_2, A_3, and λ are matrices of appropriate dimensions.

3.4. Some Practical Difficulties

There are several aspects that should be kept in perspective while operationalizing the model. In particular, there are some equally plausible alternatives at every level of specification. This is primarily a reflection of the fragmented nature of research in this area. As such the presentation is not intended to be exhaustive.

Consider the specification of the proximate objectives which a higher level manager sets for each of the divisions.

(a) The board of directors, acting on behalf of the shareholders, will be generally oriented towards maximizing the market value of the firm.

(i) However, it must be recognized that this is a consequence of certain more basic guidelines they can offer to the managers who are in charge of long term decisions. For, the proper utilization of existing assets, the acquisition of new capital, and the method of financing are equally of concern to them. In this sense the size and composition of assets, suitably defined, may be a more meaningful objective[3].

(ii) Even if the value maximization conceptualization is pursued they know that it is not possible to achieve it in practice unless the constraints placed on the management and the incentives provided to them are adequate to eliminate the adverse selection resulting from inadequate information, and the problem of moral hazard. Value maximization must be tempered by suitably choosing the constraints and incentives. That is, they may have a preference function of their own exhibiting a tradeoff between value and costs of enforcing control.

(iii) It was already noted that the board of directors may value the stability of the market share of the firm in addition to the market value. Even if the analytical objective is specified as one of determining the relative weights assigned to these goals it would be necessary to specify the channels through which the decisions alter the extent to which the objectives can be pursued. In

---

3. The usual position is that this will be an instrument or a decision which has an effect on the value of the firm. The difficulty is the absence of an objectively specied operational procedure to distinguish between goals and decisions. It is also obvious that the objectives pursued by one division may be the decisions of a different level of hierarchy within the firm.

general, there is a necessity to specify more than one G as constraints. The analytical solution appears to be straight forward if only there is a consensus on the specification from an economic and/or managerial perspective. Since economic theory cannot adequately resolve this issue there is an acute need for empirical information.

(b) The proximate objective of maximizing profit which is attributed to the marketing manager is subject to similar limitations. It is equally plausible to argue that they should be simply asked to maximize the sales volume at predetermined retail/wholesale prices.

(c) The case of the production manager is also analogous. One approach to the problem is to argue that they will be expected to make sure that the sales targets are fulfilled by an appropriate choice of production levels and inventory. However, since this is one of the major cost centers and value addition by the firm is crucially dependent on the costs of this division it is equally plausible to suggest that cost minimization should be specified as the objective. However, given the technology and production engineering practices, it would be plausible to argue that managerial discretion to increase costs at the level of the production decisions are minimal.

The basic point of this argument is that though some proximate objectives being attributed to each division appear more plausible than others there is a need for further experimentation to reduce the range of choices in the context of each of the firms. It is rather difficult to obtain precise empirical information to achieve this.

Turning to the nature of the controls or decisions at each divisional level it has been postulated that such choices are independent of each other. However, many of these choices are dependent. Consider the following examples.

(a) Given the decision on the volume of capital investment in the firm there are interdependent choices of the method of financing.

(b) For a given degree of product diversity, or more generally a corporate strategy, there are several choices of organizational structure and control mechanisms to implement it.

(c) Inventory decisions of the firm cannot be totally independent of the targeted volume of sales and the flexibility of production in adjusting to market demand.

More recent research has been highlighting such interactive effects. See, for instance, Rao and Saha (1994 a), Rediker and Seth (1995), and the references cited therein. However, from the viewpoint of the above modelling framework it is necessary to make sure that the vector of decision variables are independent of each other. The effects of their interdependence on the decision making process can be taken into account by suitably amending the specification of the constraints. Though it appears that this approach can be operationalized the specific details of specification and estimation remain elusive[4].

There is an alternative to the specification of managerial preferences or the tradeoff between the objectives. For, it is possible to argue that having gained control the management would be in a position to claim and obtain a share of the gains as perks. If this is possible, the management may yet maximize the market value of the firm. An equivalent formulation would then be for the management to maximize

$$G = A_0 + C'A_1C + C'A_2X + A_3Z + C'\lambda Y$$

and claim $C'\lambda Y$ as the payment to themselves[5].

---

4. In a somewhat unrelated context Ilmakunas (1985,1986), Wolak (1989 a,b), and others are developing estimation techniques for problems of this nature. However, this area is as yet rather new. The present study takes the interaction effects into account through $C'A_1C$ and $C'A_2X$ as specified in the previous section.

5. The important point is that this alternative specification also results in the same choices of C as the model specified in the previous section. To that extent the two specifications are equivalent. The differences between them will have to be examined from a different vantagepoint before making a choice. One approach

However, at the conceptual level, it is unrealistic to expect the management to obtain a share of the capital gains. The usual specification that they receive a part of the short run profits is more meaningful[6]. Hence, the incentive variables (Y) generally relate to the share of current profits. If the incentives are in the form of shareholding by the management the capital gains accrue as a result of ownership rather than sharing current profits. In such a case the management can be expected to alter their decisions C and accordingly the market value of the firm. The Y variables do not have an independent effect on G. In other words, a movement along the valuation frontier, as postulated in the previous section, is more plausible in comparison to a shift in it implied by this alternative.

The above argument suggests that there is a more fundamental difficulty in classifying a certain variable as belonging to a X or Y category. Consider the following examples:

(a) Suppose there is a business risk implicit in the product market conditions. Would the management place a value on this or not? The position taken in the current modelling exercise is that it is a X

---

5. (contd)

is to estimate the parameters and

(a) test the levels of significance of the parameters, and

(b) compare the values of the multiple correlation coefficients of the two formulations.

In the initial stages this approach was adopted. Invariably, the model specification of section 3.3 performed better than this alternative. The alternative is to make the decision on the basis of the underlying economic theory. This approach is preferered througout the present study.

6. The theoretical argument implies that the preferences of the management for a specific value of C has a basis other than their share of gains. For instance, the marketing manager may defend a market share for its own sake whatever may be the implications for the returns they recieve or the short run profits of the firm.

variable. For, the management knows that such changes have a fundamental bearing on the market value of the firm if they cannot adequately alter their decisions. Such changes impinge on the decision making process of the management indirectly through their effect on the valuation constraint. The management does not have any direct value for such fluctuations in business risk.

(b) The debt equity ratio choice of the management can be said to have an effect on the cost structure and therefore the market value of the firm. The effect of this C variable is accommodated through $C'A_1C$ in the G function. However, the management associates a valuation on the choice of C independent of its effect on G. For, an increase in the debt equity ratio provides them corporate control and this effect is over and above the variation in G which it entails. This is accounted for by taking one of the Y variables as a constant. The question of treating the debt equity ratio as a Z variable arises only if the management does not exhibit a preference for it. This will be obvious when the estimation procedure is outlined in the next chapter.

(c) Consider a policy parameter like the corporate profit tax. An increase in this rate has an effect on the market value of the firm. It is therefore plausible to classify it as a X variable. However, notice that as the corporate profit tax rate increases the management is aware of the fact that market value constraints are more stringent. It is expected that they will reduce the extent to which they would pursue the objective of corporate control. For, they stand to lose their jobs if the market value of the firm is reduced below a certain level of tolerance. Estimation problems, it will be clear in the next chapter, exclude the possibility of this variable being both a X and a Y. A useful judgement is to treat it as a X variable.

Referring to Fig. 3.2 let G be the valuation frontier and U the preference function. The optimal choice of C by the management is then A. Suppose the optimal choice changes to A' as and when a particular variable has changed over time. This may be a result of
(a) a shift in the valuation frontier to G' without any change in the indifference map, or
(b) a change in the managerial preferences to U^* with G remaining

invariant.

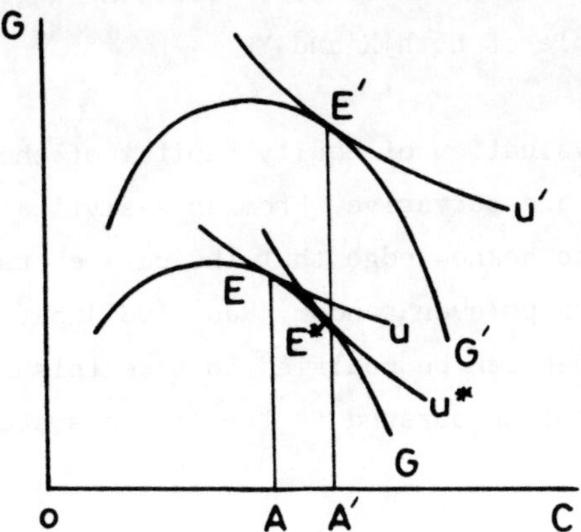

FIG. 3.2. EQUIVALENT CHANGE IN u AND G

The specification and estimation of the model should be able to distinguish between these two alternatives[7].

At the present stage the econometric procedures are not sufficiently sharp in distinguishing between these two cases[8]. The best guide is economic theory.

It should be reiterated that, at least in some cases, the

---

7. It should be observed that the identification problem in equilibrium systems is analogous. Even in that context identification is generally achieved by invoking economic theory. As in most of the other applied econometric problems the initial hypothesis is generated from the economic analysis and econometric tests used to obtain a denial or confirmation. The problem here is structurally similar.

8. Note that the possibility of a combination of these two effects operating on the choice of C cannot be ruled out apriori. That is, a specific variable may be both a X and a Y. At the present stage of analytical development models which try to accommodate both the possibilities are hopelessly underidentified.

classification is a matter of analytical judgement. The analytical structure does not have the flexibility of allowing a given variable to have the role of both X and Y.

Changes in the market valuation of equity capital of the firm and managerial preferences are pervasive. From an analytical viewpoint it would be necessary to acknowledge that the parameters of the model are variable; perhaps even random. Rao (1987) has shown that the estimation techniques can be modified to take this contingency into account. It will not be pursued further in this study.

CHAPTER 4

METHOD OF ESTIMATION

4.1. The Problem

Consider the performance of the firm or any of its divisions in particular. Generally the strategic decisions of the management as well as the market conditions external to the firm determine the level of performance. It can therefore be represented by

$$G = G(C,X)$$

where, as in chapter 3,

G = a measure of the performance of the firm,

C = the choice or decision of the management, and

X = a market related variable (e.g., the market demand for the product of the firm).

The management of the firm chooses a (G,C) combination out of this feasible set.

In general, the strategic choices of the management depend not only on the performance criterion but also on the incentives and constraints defined by the higher level management or the board of directors as the case may be. Since the latter set of variables do not enter the market valuation they must be influencing the managerial decisions through their preference function. That is, the management may be conceptualized as choosing C so as to maximize

$$U = U(G,C,Y)$$

where the level of U depends upon the performance measured by G, the preference which the management associates with C, and Y represents the incentives (e.g., the wages and salaries and perks) and the constraints (e.g., the dividends per share) which the management must take into account.

The optimal choice of C will then be

$$C = C(X,Y)$$

See, for instance, Fig.4.1. However, it is obvious that the

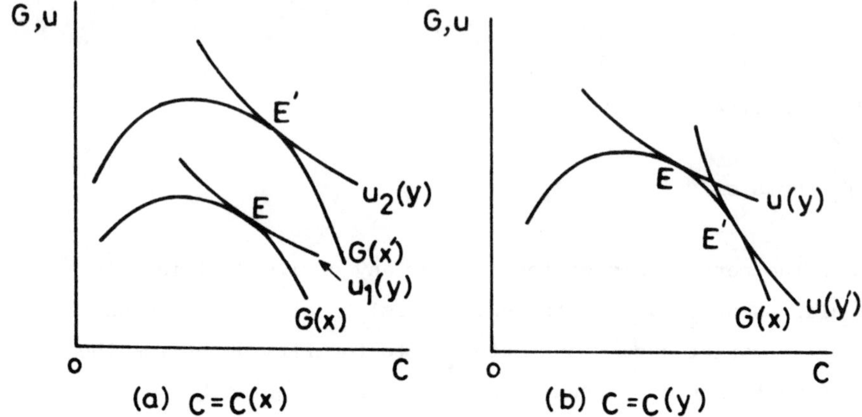

FIG.4.1. VARIATIONS IN C WITH x AND y

specification of the G and U functions leave considerable scope with respect to the specification of the

(a) hierarchy of decisions,

(b) incentives and constraints on the decision making at each level, and

(c) extent to which the information contained in the observed value of C can be used to infer the nature of the G and U functions.

In general, it should be noted that it is possible to observe the changes in G and C (but not U) as X and Y vary. The empirical problem is to estimate the parameters of the G and U functions from these observations.

Many unsuccessful attempts have been made to estimate such models. Lintner (1971, p.218), in particular, pointed out that the knowledge regarding managerial preferences remained incomplete since it has not been possible to estimate the relative weights which the management assigns to value increasing objectives and other aspects which they take into account. More recently, Schmalensee (1989, p.957) acknowledged that the " data on endogenous variables (i.e., the actual choices of the management) do provide the information, though not the sort that can be handled by commonly employed estimation techniques." Radice (1971, p.549), and Cubbin and Leech (1986, p.124) recognized the existence of an identification problem which must be resolved.

It can be shown that the estimation methods available in the literature are unsatisfactory due to an inappropriate choice of the economic basis from which the requisite information can be extracted. Section 4.2 sets out the essential details since the present study represents a fundamental departure from the existing methods of estimation.

Section 4.3 offers a theoretically justifiable alternative specification of the method of estimation which resolves the identification problem in a simple case. Section 4.4 provides a generalization of these results to a case where the management makes many decisions. Section 4.5 outlines some of the practical difficulties which need attention while implementing the algorithm.

4.2. The Current Status[1]

It was noted in chapter 3 that the model specification usually takes the form

---

1. Early attempts at testing such hypotheses utilized reduced form specifications. That is, they write

$C = C(X,Y)$

$G = G(X,Y)$

and estimate the parameters of these reduced form equations. Such studies do not deserve any serious consideration since they do not postulate any well defined model from which this reduced form can be derived. Instead, as Mueller (1967, pp.59-60) put it, " in writing each equation the researcher makes explicit assumptions only regarding the variables the entrepreneur considers relevant for each decision and not about the motives behind these decisions. One's perception regarding the goals of the firm are often introduced via the selection of the predetermined variables to be included in each equation." Even the best known study of Grabowski and Mueller (1972) can be classified only in this

$$G = a_0 + a_1 C^2 + a_2 X$$

$$U = G + \lambda_1 C + \lambda_2 Y$$

The estimation methods currently in vogue deal with this specification alone. An attempt will be made at the outset to outline the basic difficulties associated with the available methods of estimation.

The first basic approach to the problem started with the observation that the convexity of the preference function (indicating the manager's willingness to forego a certain amount of G to achieve a higher C) would result in a negative correlation between the observed values[2] of G and C as in Fig.4.2. Radice

---

1. (contd)

category. Such specifications do not capture the essential aspects of managerial discretion. Further, they are also valid even if the management pursues value maximization as the only objective. As a result they cannot offer any insight into the nature of managerial preferences. See, for instance, Mueller (1986, p.164) and Schmalensee (1988, p.672).

2. The following presentation of McConnell and Muscarella (1985, p.20) is typical. "Under the size maximization hypothesis, managers seek to increase the size of the firm. Thus, they are lead to overinvest in capital projects. That is, they invest beyond the point where marginal returns equal the market required returns. The empirical prediction of the size maximization hypothesis is that unexpected increases in capital expenditures should have a negative impact on the market value of the firm and unexpected decreases in capital expenditures should have a positive impact on the market value of the firm. The empirical results of this paper (at least, on an average) are consistent with the market value maximization, and they are inconsistent with the size maximization hypothesis." Tests of hypotheses regarding other managerial preferences adopted a similar approach. Studies

(1971), working with the Marris (1964) model, observed a positive correlation and concluded that the postulated managerial preferences do not exist.

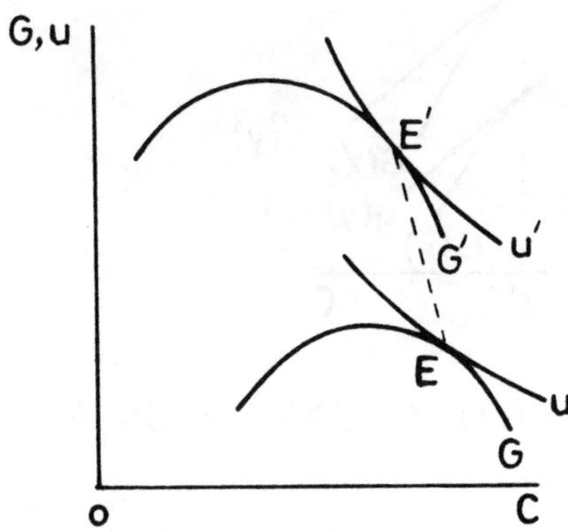

FIG.4.2. NEGATIVE CORRELATION BETWEEN G AND C

However, this inference is erroneous for two reasons. Firstly, the above model specification indicates that the optimal value of C is

$$C^{*} = -(\lambda_1/2a_1)$$

whatever may be the values of X and Y. As a result the expansion path, which is a representation of the optimal (G,C) choices as X and Y vary, will be a vertical line through C^{*} as represented in Fig.4.3. There is no possibility of obtaining any negative correlation between the observed values of G and C. Secondly, even in a more general model there is no basis for the expectation that the locus of the observed (G,C) values would be negatively sloped if $\lambda_1 > 0$. For, as Fig.4.4 indicates, a positive slope is as likely as a negative slope.

The second approach was suggested by Cubbin and Leech (1986, p.126). They argued that all the parameters of the model can be estimated if the valuation frontier, viz.,

---

2. (contd)

of Marby and Siders (1967), Edwards (1977), and Mester (1989) provide a representative sample.

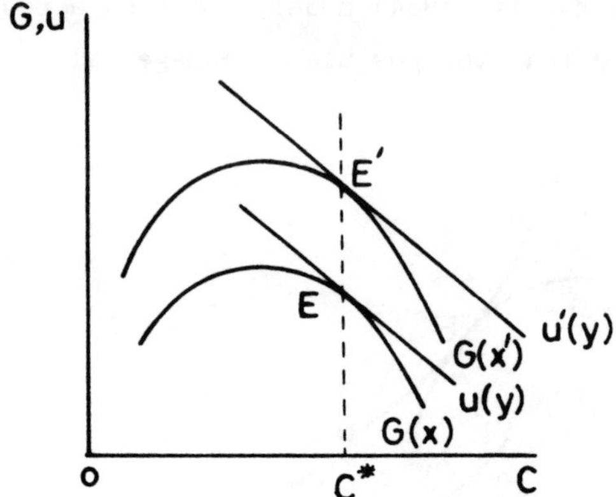

FIG.4.3. A VERTICAL EXPANSION PATH

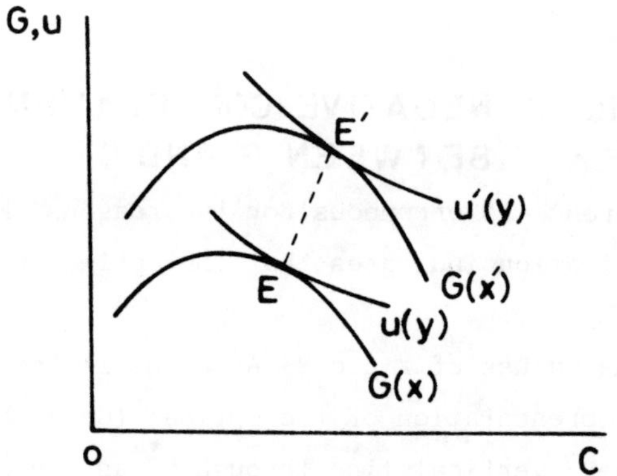

FIG.4.4. POSITIVELY SLOPED EXPANSION PATH

$G = G(C, X)$

and the expansion path (i.e., the locus of the ex post choices of C and the resulting G) are considered as a system of equations.

For the above model, in particular, the valuation frontier is

$$G = a_0 + a_1 C^2 + a_2 X$$

The expansion path can be obtained by substituting the optimality condition for the choice of C in the above equation. Note that

$2a_1 C + \lambda_1 = 0$

so that

$a_1 C = - a_1 C - \lambda_1$

resulting in

$$G = a_0 - a_1 C^2 - \lambda_1 C + a_2 X$$

However, these two equations do not represent a simultaneous system of equations. In addition, since $C = C^*$ (a constant) independent of X and Y, the expansion path can be written as

$$G = a_0 + a_1 C^2 + a_2 X$$

$$= a_0^* + a_2 X$$

Hence, it can be concluded that

(a) the parameters a_0 and a_1 cannot be estimated independently, and

(b) λ_2 is not estimable even if it is assumed that λ_1 can be estimated.

In effect, neither the valuation frontier nor the expansion path are identifiable. It is not surprising that the empirical work of Cubbin and Leech (1986) did not yield any meaningful estimates of either of these equations.

A natural question will now be this. Will these methods of estimation be satisfactory if the alternative specification proposed in chapter 3 is adopted? Let the valuation frontier be

$$G = a_0 + a_1C^2 + a_2CX$$

and the preference function be

$$U = G + \lambda_1C + \lambda_2CY$$

Observe that this modification results in the first order condition

$$2a_1C + a_2X + \lambda_1 + \lambda_2Y = 0$$

and the optimal choice

$$C^* = b_1X + b_{20} + b_{21}Y$$

where $b_1 = -(a_2/2a_1)$, $b_{20} = -(\lambda_1/2a_1)$, and $b_{21} = -(\lambda_2/2a_1)$.

The expansion path implicit in the alternative specification is

$$G = a_0 - a_1C^2 - \lambda_1C - \lambda_2CY$$

so that the slope of the expansion path is

$$dG/dC = -\lambda_1 - 2a_1C - \lambda_2Y$$

which, given the optimality condition, reduces to

$$dG/dC = a_2X$$

This does not exclude the possibility of the expansion path being positively sloped. In other words, even this alternative specification indicates that the negative slope of the expansion path is neither necessary nor sufficient to conclude that there is a managerial preference for C.

Similarly, the valuation frontier and the expansion path implied by the alternative specification are identifiable if they constitute a system of equations. However, given the optimality condition, both of them reduce to a single equation

$$G = a_0 + a_1(Y^{*2} - X^{*2})$$

where $X^* = b_1X$, and $Y^* = b_{20} + b_{21}Y$

It can be concluded that the Cubbin and Leech (1986) procedure is inadequate even in the context of the alternative specification[3,4].

4.3. The Proposed Estimation Procedure

The appropriate method of estimation can be motivated in the following manner. Consider the economic basis underlying the managerial decisions. Let the change in the market variables (X) and the managerial considerations (Y) be given. Firstly, for any change in C which the management conceptualizes they have an idea regarding the likely changes in the market valuation of their decisions and their level of satisfaction. The optimal choice of C reflects this information. Hence, it is possible to estimate the parameters b_1, b_{20}, and b_{21} from the optimality condition. However, the management's choice of C does not depend on the position of the valuation frontier (i.e., the value of the parameter a_0). The parameter a_0 must be estimated from some other source. The valuation frontier is inadequate for this purpose since it postulates the effect on G of an ex ante change in the value of C independent of the changes in X and Y. However, the

---

3. Since the Cubbin and Leech (1986) procedure does not specify a method of estimating the parameters b_{20} and b_{21} it must be concluded that a_1 and a_2 cannot be identified. In other words, their method is inadequate even in the context of the alternative specification.

4. The nature of the identification problem in models of decision making under uncertainty is somewhat distinct though it is similar to the problem encountered in the specification of equilibrium systems. Rao (1988 a,b,1994), Rao and Singh (1987, 1990 a,b), and Rao, Singh, and Talwar (1991 a,b) examined such problems extensively.

observed variations in C are primarily a result of the market conditions and the managerial preferences. It is these decisions C which in their turn determine the observed changes in the market value of the decisions. In general, all the ex post variations in G are along the expansion path. That is, the reduced form specification of the expansion path contains the information about the parameter a_0 though the optimality constraint does not. Rothenberg (1971,pp.584-5) recognized this aspect of the identification problem explicitly.

Returning to the equation for the expansion path it should be noted that all the parameters of the model will be identifiable only if a_1 is estimable. As noted in Rao (1988 a,b), Rao and Singh (1987,1990 a,b), and Rao, Singh and Talwar (1991 a,b) this is a general problem of estimation in models of this nature. Fortunately, the reduced form specification of the expansion path makes a_0, a_1, and a_3 estimable since X^*, and Y^* can be estimated from the optimality condition. In general, the reduced form specification of the expansion path contains the requisite information about all the parameters of the model which the optimality constraint does not. No identification problem is encountered in this simple problem if the proposed method of estimation is adopted[5].

---

5. Note that a constant term is not included in the specification of a_1^*. This is motivated by the requirements of estimation as well. Suppose, to the contrary, that a constant α is included in a_1^*. Then the U function contains a term $(\alpha + \lambda_1)C$. As a result the value of C which maximizes U contains $(\alpha + \lambda_1)$. It would not be possible to identify the reason for this choice of C. For, α indicates that it is necessitated by the market valuation of C whereas λ_1 suggests that it is a consequence of the managerial preferences. The identification problem cannot be resolved. It is necessary to specify apriori that either $\alpha = 0$ or $\lambda_1 = 0$. It is perhaps more realistic to consider α to be zero in the context of a test of the models.

Note that the specification of the functional forms of the model is approximate. Hence, the valuation frontier should contain an error term to represent this. Further, working with certain dynamic formulations, Chow (1983,p.381) justified the inclusion of a random residual to represent "errors in the execution of optimal policy." Hence, the equation representing the optimal choice of C can be written as

$$C = b_1X + b_{20} + b_{21}Y + \varepsilon$$

where ε is a random residual[6].

Following Rao (1965, section 6a.2, p.322) each of the estimators will be asymptotically normally distributed.

The R^2 value (corrected suitably for the degrees of freedom) obtained from the regression for the expansion path can be viewed as a comprehensive measure of the goodness of fit of the overall model of managerial preferences since it embodies the information contained in both the equations of the model.

4.4. Further Generalization

In the general context C would be only one of the many variables which the management chooses. Hence, it would be more realistic to consider C as a vector of decisions. The following general model will now be considered.

$$G = A_0 + C'A_1C + C'A_2X + A_3Z, \text{ and}$$

$$U = G + C'\lambda Y$$

with the notations already defined in chapter 3.

The optimal choice of C would then satisfy the equation

---

6. Chow (1983,pp.377 ff) <u>assumed</u> that the parameters of the valuation frontier are estimable apriori and that λ_1 and λ_2 can be estimated from the expansion path. This is generally not possible.

$$2A_1C + A_2X + \lambda Y = 0$$

Further, the maximization of U requires A_1 to be negative definite. Hence, the optimal choices of managerial controls are governed by the equation

$$C = B_1X + B_2Y$$

where

$$A_2 = - 2A_1B_1, \text{ and } \lambda = - 2A_1B_2$$

However, it is as yet necessary to examine the estimability of the parameters of the expansion path.

Based on the argument of Rothenberg (1971) noted earlier, it is necessary to consider the reduced form structure. Rewrite the optimality condition in the form

$$2A_1C = - A_2X - \lambda Y$$

The expansion path can therefore be written as

$$G = A_0 + (1/2)\ (C'A_2X - C'\lambda Y) + A_3Z$$

Substituting the optimal choice of C into this equation and simplifying yields

$$G = A_0 + (1/2)\ (X'B_1'A_2X - Y'B_2'\lambda Y) + A_3Z$$

For, it is evident that

$$X'B_1'\lambda Y = Y'B_2A_2X = - 2X'B_1'A_1B_2Y$$

It is therefore necessary to estimate A_0, A_2, and λ from the expansion path.

It should be noted that the parameters appearing in the expansion path are non-linear functions of A_1, A_2, and λ of the original model. For problems of this nature Rothenberg (1971,pp.585-6) and Magnus and Neudecker (1988,p.337) offer only stiff sufficient conditions for local identification.

However, a rather general necessary and sufficient condition can be developed for the specific problem under consideration. Since A_2 is a pxq matrix and λ is a pxr matrix identifiability of A_2 and λ requires that both B_1X and B_2Y should contain p independent linear combinations of X and Y respectively. A necessary and sufficient condition for this is that

$$p \leq \text{minimum } (q,r)$$

Hence, all the parameters of the general model are identifiable if and only if this condition is satisfied.

For estimation purposes the reduced form specification of the expansion path turned out to be more efficient. Utilizing the optimality condition and the equation for the valuation frontier it can be verified that the expansion path reduces to

$$G = A_0 + Y'B_2'A_1B_2Y - X'B_1'A_1B_1X + A_3Z$$

so that A_1 can be estimated from this equation and A_2 and λ can be calculated from

$$A_2 = -2A_1B_1, \text{ and } \lambda = -2A_1B_2$$

Note that it is generally not possible to seperate all the Z variables from the X and Y variables apriori. A practical approach would be to initially estimate the C equations and reclassify all the X and Y variables which do not appear in these equations in the Z category.

4.5. Problems of Inference

In addition there are several issues of judgement in the

application of the general model specification. The following aspects need attention.

(a) problems of interpreting the results,

(b) classification of the X,Y variables,

(c) model specification for managerial preferences,

(d) inference procedures, and

(e) policy issues as implied by the modelling exercise.

In general, following the revealed preference logic, the choices would reflect

(a) the preferences of the decision makers, or

(b) the fact that the constraints are binding.

Hence, the following possibilities should be kept in perspective while interpreting the results.

(a) Good market prospects and the flexibility of the constraints may enable the decision makers to pursue several objectives simultaneously. In such a case all the square terms of the C variables will appear in the value function with a negative sign. Similarly, all the C variables will have a positive sign in the preference function.

(b) There is a possibility that the pursuit of preferences with respect to all the decisions is not in the interest of the management. For example, pursuing a widely diversified policy and financing mostly by debt may be extremely risky. The firm may still pursue one of the objectives and operate on the increasing portion of the valuation frontier with respect to others. The variables C_r, C_r^2, or C_rC_i, where C_i are the preferred decisions and C_r the rest of the C variables, will appear in the value function. It will be shown in the sequel that these will be interpreted as the strong bonding effects. However, when the pattern identified in (a) above holds only the positive sign on the interaction variables denotes the bonding effects.

(c) On occasions the market prospects may not be encouraging to a point where the management cannot indulge in any of its preferences. Instead, they may be operating on the increasing portion of the valuation frontier. In such cases it would not be possible to estimate the valuation frontier and the preference function independently. The estimated G function can only represent the expansion path. For, the second order condition for maximum will not be satisfied and the equation,

$$C = B_1X + B_2Y$$

though estimable, will lose its significance in so far as it does not contain adequate information about the parameters A and λ.

The second issue is the difficulty in classifying a given set of variables as C,X, or Y. In particular, suppose there is a business risk implicit in the product market conditions. Would the management place a value on this or not? The empirical work in the subsequent chapters will classify this as a X variable. For, the management knows that such changes have a fundamental bearing on the performance of the firm if they cannot adequately alter their decisions. The management values such a risk only to the extent it has an effect on the valuation constraint. Similarly, note that some of the Y variables are decisions of a higher level manager. Hence, they are endogenous to the system. A similar argument can be presented in the context of government policy variables which will be classified as X variables in the empirical work reported in the subsequent chapters. It can also be argued that the market variables (X) may also be influenced by the choice of C. In other words, there are wide ranging interrelationships between C, X, and Y. The classification of these variables as either endogenous or exogenous is an analytical judgement based on the specific purpose for which the model is constructed. There is a more difficult problem implied in this argument. Just as a decision model was formulated for C a similar model reflecting the decisions of the board in their choice of Y should be formulated. The simultaneous estimation of such models would be a formidable task.

The possibility of pervasive simultaneity also suggests that the adjustments in C and Y may not be instantaneous. Perhaps it would be more realistic to consider the lagged values of C and Y as well. At the present stage of analytical development it is difficult to visualize the necessary changes in the estimation procedures.

Two further aspects complicate the estimation process.

(a) Changes in the market valuation of the firm's decisions and the management's preferences are pervasive. From an analytical viewpoint it would be necessary to acknowledge that the parameters of the model are variable; perhaps even random. Rao (1988 a) has shown that the estimation techniques can be modified to take this contingency into account.

(b) Observe that the strategic decisions are represented by the reduced form, i.e.,

$$C = B_1X + B_2Y$$

they will have the form of Zellner's seemingly unrelated regressions. It may be useful to modify the estimation procedure accordingly.

Consider the policy implications of this study. Since the ultimate purpose is to devise incentives and constraints to attain the maximum possible market value it would be natural to investigate the reasons why the choices of Y by the board of directors is not optimal. From a conceptual viewpoint the choices of the management would coincide with the maximum market value if and only if $\lambda Y = 0$. For, if this condition is satisfied the maximum U is the same as the maximum G irrespective of the choice of C. Since the specification of Y contains a constant it is possible to write

$Y' = (1\ Y^{*\prime})$, and

$\lambda = (\lambda_0\ \lambda^{*})$

so that

$$\lambda^{*}Y^{*} = -\lambda_0$$

This can be solved uniquely for Y^{*} if and only if $p = (r-1)$, and λ^{*} is non-singular. Hence, in general, it is difficult to ascertain the optimality of Y chosen by the board. The policy issue should be considered afresh.

CHAPTER 5

OPERATIONALIZING THE MODEL

5.1. The Data Base

The empirical results of the present study pertain to the chemical industry in the corporate sector. It is based on the time series data for 27 firms[1]. The basic sources of the data are the balance sheets and the profit and loss accounts of these companies as published in the various issues of the Bombay Stock Exchange official directory.

No specific sampling design was used for selecting the firms. Instead, all the firms, for which at least 20 years of data between 1967-94 was available for all the relevant variables, were included.

The rest of the chapter is organized as follows. Section 5.2 reproduces, in a summary fashion, the definitions provided in the stock exchange official directory. Section 5.3 describes the measurement of the variables and the rationale for the specific choices made. Section 5.4 outlines certain basic limitations of the published data and the difficulties associated with obtaining primary data on the relevant variables.

5.2. Some Accounting Definitions

The explanatory notes of the Bombay Stock Exchange official directory provide the information about the construction of items and the interpretation of the data of a company under the following heads:

(a) comparative financial statements

(b) common-size financial statements

---

1. The list of the firms is presented at the beginning of the book.

(c) trend percentage

(d) ratios of items selected from the balance sheet and the profit and loss statements and from both the statements taken together

(e) equity data

The requisite definitions provided therein are reproduced for convenient reference.

(a) Book value per share

It represents the investment per share made in the business by the shareholders. In other words, it represents on a per share basis the net assets (excluding intangibles) after offsetting all the liabilities against the assets. It can be defined as

$B = A + (R - I - D)/E$

where

B = book value per share

A = amount called up per share

R = shareholders' reserves

I = intangible assets

D = preference dividends in arrears

E = number of equity shares subscribed.

(b) The market price to book value

This ratio represents the market valuation of every rupee of equity of the company. It represents the extent to which the market value of the equity is justified on the basis of the book value of the assets of the company. The ratio is defined as

$M = P/B$

where

M = the ratio of the market price to book value

P = average market price of the month in which the company's financial year ends

B = book value per share

(c) Net sales

This is calculated by deducting goods returned, allowances, and discounts from the gross amount received from sales.

(d) Net profit

By definition

Net profit = pre-tax profit - provision for taxation

Pre-tax profit = operating profit + non-operating surplus earned from activities outside the basic business of the firm

Operating profit = gross profit - depreciation allowance - long term and short term interest charges

Gross profit = sales revenue - cost of goods sold

Cost of goods sold = costs of production and general expenses

(e) Inventory

Inventory comprises of goods held for sale or in the process of manufacture and supplies of inputs which are necessary to operate the business. In the case of manufacturing firms the item is subdivided into raw materials, semifinished, and finished goods.

(f) Interest payments

Interest payments include interest paid on debentures, bonds, and borrowed funds.

(g) Liquidity ratio

The liquidity ratio, commonly referred to as the current ratio, provides a test of solvency and determines the short term financial strength. A ratio of 2:1 is considered satisfactory. For, it indicates that even if the value of the current assets were to shrink to one half the creditors would receive payment in full. However, a high liquidity ratio does not necessarily imply better liquidity. It is necessary to consider it in conjunction with the varying quality and characteristics of the current assets. By definition

Liquidity ratio = current assets/current liabilities

(h) Provisions for taxation provides an indirect check on the reported earnings. Weak companies tend to understate their tax liabilities, whereas an excess provision is made by some companies which do not wish to disclose to the shareholders the larger profits they have earned. The tax provision in the profit and loss statement should be compared with the tax payable, as calculated at the prescribed rates, on the earnings reported in the statement. In many cases, there would be a significant difference between the two. The difference may be due to special provisions in the tax statutes, such as lower tax rates applicable to initial slabs, tax free interest income from gilt-edged securities, less tax payable on intercorporate dividends, carry forward of losses, or accelerated depreciation allowed for developmental purposes to specific industries etc.

(i) General expenses
Selling expenses include selling, administrative, and other indirect expenses not related to the cost of producing goods.

(j) Cost of goods sold
The cost of goods sold contains stocks consumed, wages and salaries, and direct manufacturing expenses.

(k) Dividends per share
Dividends per share represent the actual amount of dividend (gross) declared per share of common stock.

Some of the data provided in the accounts of the firm are directly usable for the analytical purposes of the present study. The rest of the variables had to be constructed from the available data. The details will be presented in the next section.

5.3. The Variables

On the basis of the theoretical specification of the model, as outlined in chapter 3, section 3, the variables can be broadly classified in the following manner.

(a) The variables representing the targets of the managers of the different divisions

(b) The decision variables at each of the levels of decision making

(c) The market related variables

(d) The government policy variables

(e) the incentives and constraints

(f) The Z variables

The basic long term performance measure considered in the study is the market value of the firm. It reflects the shareholder valuation of the physical assets of the firm. As such it represents a constraint on the long term decisions of the firm. It is estimated by

MAVA = market value of the firm (Rs.crores)

= valuation ratio x book value of common stock + preference capital + long term loans + debentures

where

valuation ratio = market price of a unit of common stock/ book value

The reasoning behind this measurement is as follows.

(a) Suppose the capital assets of the firm are liquidated at any point of time. The market price offered for the common stock depends upon the assessed market potential and the value of the capital assets. However, the total value of assets should be equal to the total liabilities[2]. Hence, the market value of the firm is computed by taking all the long term liabilities into account.

(b) The sale proceeds will be utilized to payoff debentures and long term loans in the first instance. The next priority is to pay the preference shareholders. Further, in most cases, the market price offered for the common stock on the capital market is an adequate reflection of the remaining market value of the firm. Given this assumption the valuation ratio can accurately capture the market valuation of the physical capital of the firm after making allowance for the other liabilities.

---

2. Current liabilities have not been taken into account for two reasons:

(a) it would be unusual for short term creditors to have a claim on the capital assets of the firm, and

(b) it is generally expected that the current assets are sufficiently large and adequate to pay for the current liabilities.

However, note that as reported in the stock exchange directory the book value of the firm makes an allowance for the shareholders' reserves. Hence, this item of liabilities has not been included in the calculation of the market value of the firm.

The vice president in charge of short run operations of the firm evaluates the decisions of the managers of the different divisions of the firm on specific and specialized objectives. In particular, the following details should be noted.

(a) The marketing manager has the best market information. Normally he would be expected to set a target for the market share of the different products of the firm. Since most firms fix retail prices apriori it can be expected that such sales targets maximize the sales revenue. However, the vice president can generally calibrate the cost implications of the market share strategy. Hence, he can evaluate the decisions of this manager in terms of the profits of the firm. Effectively, the marketing manager considers the implications of his decisions for net profits as one of the constraints. The appropriate objective for this division is therefore

NPRO = net profits of the firm (Rs.crores)

(b) The production manager has the more specific job of organizing production in such a way that the sales targets can be fulfilled. Hence, the proximate objective for this division is

NSAL = net sales (Rs.crores)

(c) For all practical purposes the roles of the personnel and financial managers are complementary to those of the production manager. No other specific goals are conceptualized for them in the present modelling effort[3].

---

3. In some early rounds of the investigation an attempt was made to assign to the financial manager the role of minimizing the cost of financing the working capital requirements. However, this did not yield any satisfactory results. For all practical purposes, this may be a result of one of the following.

(a) Assuming that the demand curves for the products of the firm are sufficiently inelastic most of the cost increases can be passed on to the consumer. If this is valid then the financial

The major long term decisions of the firm are

(a) GRTH = rate of growth of capital assets

= [net assets at t - net assets at (t-1)]/ net assets at (t-1)

expressed as a percentage

where

t = a specific interval of time (year).

(b) DEBT = debt equity ratio[4]

The instruments available to the managers in the short run also differ from one division to another.

(a) The marketing manager decides NSAL as defined above, and/or

GNEX = advertising and promotion campaigns

= selling costs/ cost of goods sold

For, given the market uncertainties, he realizes that every market share choice must be defended by appropriate marketing strategies.

(b) The production manager[5], in consultation with the personnel manager, chooses

---

3. (contd)

manager's job is to raise the necessary finances by choosing a suitable portfolio. Cost considerations will be secondary.

(b) It has been often claimed that the credit limits and working capital norms defined by the banking system are rigid and binding. Even in this case the financial managers of the firm cannot have such a choice even if they aim at cost minimization.

4. Note that, following Turnovsky (1970, p.1065), the debt equity ratio was defined in terms of the book value rather than the market value.

5. To the production manager NSAL represents the valuation of his decisions by the vice president of operations. The NSAL is the expected supply given the decisions of the production manager. The NSAL decision of the marketing manager can be viewed as a demand he places on the production manager.

INSA = inventory to sales ratio

= end of period inventory/ net sales

and/or

WASA = wages and salaries/ cost of goods sold

In general, these choices depend on the extent to which production is flexible ex post.

The characterization of the market environment is subject to one basic limitation. For, as Whittington (1988, p.250), and Lyles and Schwenk (1992, p.157 ff) put it, it is not easy to define the market environment the way it is. It can be assessed only to the extent that such distinctive competencies have been built up by the management over time. In other words, an ex ante specification of the market environment is impractical. Instead, the observed values must be used as a proxy for the ex ante expectations. Further, the specification of the market related variables depends on the context. In the long run decision process NSAL[6] and NPRO[7] are two such measures. In addition, the following variables are taken into account.

NFAS = net fixed assets (Rs.crores)[8]

---

6. It can be argued that information about gross sales is more appropriate. However, it includes the goods returned, allowances, and discounts to the distributors. Hence, net sales may be the more appropriate variable while assessing the operating income on which the profit or loss accrues.

7. Gross profit is not relevant to the appraisal of the firm's performance. For, suppose the debt is large. Then a large portion of gross profits is utilized to make the interest payments and has the effect of restricting value adding activities. In general, the net profit is the more appropriate measure in the decision making context.

8. The literature indicates the importance of the effect of the net fixed assets on the compensation policy alone. It is therefore possible that net sales, rather than net fixed assets, provides a better proxy for the size of the firm.

Business risk is the other major variable representing the market environment. Turnovsky (1970, p.1064), and Vickers (1987, pp.162-3) characterize the business risk as the variability in the demand for various products of the firm when the product markets are uncertain. For purposes of the present study it has been defined in terms of the degree of instability in the firm's net operating income[9].

BSRI = business risk

= absolute value of [{net sales at t - net sales at (t-1)}/ net sales at t]

Turnovsky (1970) considers the financial risk as an additional risk to the shareholders as a consequence of the use of borrowed funds. In general, it should be noted that an increase in the debt equity ratio increases the rate of interest on borrowed funds. This creates a more than proportionate increase in the interest payments. A larger proportion of net sales will then be necessary to cover the interest obligations since the interest payments are, for all practical purposes, a fixed cost. An uncertain product market aggrevates the financial risk implicit in the choice of a high debt equity ratio[10]. The financial risk[11] is therefore measured by

FIRI = financial risk

= interest payments/ net sales

---

9. Note that conceptually a measure of variance of net sales at time t would be the appropriate measure of business risk. Since this cannot be measured in a convenient fashion the procedure adopted here is the best approximation.

10. It is unrealistic to expect the debt equity ratio to serve the role of financial risk. For, the latter is a flow measure for each interval of time. On the other hand, the debt equity ratio captures the bankruptcy risk involved in the liquidation of the capital assets at a point of time. Even in the long run, a high debt equity ratio captures the financial risk given the expected product market conditions. It cannot indicate the nature of the product market conditions per se.

Generally the government policy is one of the dimensions of the environment in which the firm operates. As such it can be argued that the variables which capture the effect of the government policy are also X variables. In other words, their effect on the performance of the firm is one of the main reasons for the changes in the strategic decisions of the management. The following policy variables have been included in the present study.

The most important policy measure is the corporate profit tax rate. It is defined as

TAXT = taxation rate

= provision for taxation/ pre-tax profit

Short term liquidity problems for financing working capital have been extensively documented in the context of the corporate sector. The working capital shortage reduces the production potential and makes it difficult to convert fixed assets to profits. This liquidity position is measured by

LIQD = liquidity ratio

= current assets/ current liabilities

Incentives and constraints are the most important set of Y variables which affect the decision making process of the

---

11. An alternative measure of financial risk is

FIRI = interest payments/ gross profits

This would have been a better choice because interest is paid from the gross profit. But there is a practical difficulty with this measure. Suppose the gross profit is negative. Then, even if the interest burden is low it does not mean that the firm is not facing a financial risk. Instead, the firm has to either borrow from the money market or divert resources from its reserves and surpluses account to make the interest payment. On the other hand, net sales cannot be negative.

management[12]. These variables have been operationalized as follows.

Wages and salaries is one of the elements of the compensation package offered to the management. Its impact on the decision making can be reflected by
WASA = wages and salaries/ cost of goods sold

As DeAlessi and Fishe (1987, p.41) put it, the shareholders may insist on regular dividend payments to reduce the need to monitor the management. For, the retention of earnings gives the management an opportunity to divert resources to their advantage even if they continue to make investments which increase the market value of the firm. The conventional measure of such a constraint on the management is
DIND = dividends per share (in Rs.)

Turning to the Z variables it should be recognized that all the above mentioned X and Y variables qualify as Z variables. For, as specified in chapter 3, section 3, all the variables which the decision makers consider very expensive to adjust to in their decision making will be reclassified as Z variables.

However, one observation is noteworthy. The specification of the G function in chapter 3, section 3, clearly indicates that any X variable which does not affect the C decision would nevertheless have an effect on G. Can a similar hypothesis be maintained with respect to the Y variables? Consider WASA. Assume that the management is not willing to exhibit any weak bonding effect in

---

12. Managerial shareholding can be considered as one of the incentives provided to the management for the alignment of their objectives with those of the shareholders. Rao and Saha (1994 a,b), and Rao, Rastogi, and Saha (1995) included this variable in crosssection studies. However, it was not taken into account in the present study due to the non-availability of the data on a time series basis.

their decision making. Even in such a case an increase in WASA represents a cost to the firm and has an effect on G. The higher level managers can be expected to view the increase in WASA from this vantage point especially in situations where the weak bonding effect is not discrenible. On the other hand, they may not consider it as reducing G if a weak bonding effect is exhibited. Similarly, assume that an increase in DIND does not result in the expected bonding effect. The higher level management may then feel that the reductions in the cashflow may reduce the level of G attained. In other words, there is a conceptual possibility that the Y variables have the role of Z variables in the absence of weak bonding effects.

5.4. Some Limitations

Empirical research regarding economic behavior within organizations is as yet relatively new. Most of the information utilized in the earlier studies is for a cross section of firms within an industry or across industries. Further, most of the studies assemble the empirical data from primary sources, i.e., directly from the firms. In general, much of the requisite information cannot be obtained from any secondary or published sources. This is a severe limitation and restricts the range of issues that can be examined. Usually such cross section studies are inadequate to obtain information about discretionary managerial behavior because there will be fundamental differences across firms. Further, there can be differences across different divisions of a given firm depending on the organizational culture. This level of detailed empirical work is fairly difficult.

The present study is an attempt to use published sources of information to initiate some research into this area. As such there are several limitations from the empirical perspective which add on to the difficulties from the theoretical perspective. This section is intended to highlight a few major issues.

The chairman's statements of most of the companies indicate that certain broad environmental aspects like product diversification, relationship with distribution and marketing outlets, joint ventures, foreign equity participation, unforeseen hazards and so on affect their decisions and performance significantly. However, it has not been possible to make any quantitative appraisal of such influences. While conducting the analysis of managerial decisions environmental factors which each of them confront are different. A variable, like the business risk defined in the present study, may only have a limited effect on the production decisions of the firm to the extent that it is acting as a proxy for the fluctuations in the net sales targets given to them. It is equally important to acknowlege that the managerial decisions of any one divisional level will depend on the organizational culture, e.g., the operation of the quality circles, just-in-time and so on. Such effects of organizational structure will be generally cumulative over time. However, it is difficult to define the quantitative content of such organizational influences as they affect the decisions of the divisional managers and the performance of specific divisions.

The present study takes the position that managerial preferences for growth of capital assets, inventory, general expenses and such other quantifiable variables are adequate to reflect their priorities. However, as Marginson (1985) and others pointed out, a divisional manager and the workers of the division may develop self serving relationships and preferences which cannot be fully captured by the above variables. Even a proper description of these possibilities is as yet quite elusive.

Some problems are a result of the nature and extent of the decision making powers at the divisional level. In particular, consider the decisions of the production manager. Without detailed information it is difficult to say whether or not they have the autonomy to choose appropriate financing for working capital. Even if they do the financial risk defined in this study reflects the firm level risk and may be inadequate to capture the divisional effect. Further, it does not seperate the risks associated with the short term financing from those related to long term portfolio choice.

The issues involved in the specification of incentives offered to the managers and the constraints placed on them are similar. In particular, it is reasonable to postulate that they will be different depending on the divisional needs. However, the present study utilizes measures like the wages and salaries and dividends per share which relate to the company as a whole and not to any of its divisions in particular. Neither the conceptual basis nor the empirical information is available to improve upon this specification.

These limitations must be kept in perspective while interpreting the results in the subsequent chapters.

CHAPTER 6

INVESTMENTS AND CAPITAL STRUCTURE

6.1. The Strategic Choices

The modern corporation operates in an inherently uncertain dynamic environment where a number of competing firms are making attempts to serve expanding markets with a view to

(a) increasing their profits, and

(b) capturing an ever increasing market share.

Since the emphasis is on the long term prospects each firm endeavors to anticipate the emerging market trends ahead of others, identify profitable investments, and implement them efficiently. See, for instance, Filippi and Zanetti (1971,pp.147 ff), and Lintner (1971,p.172).

However, diffused shareholding implies that it is not possible to have a coherent group of shareholders who

(a) have adequate knowledge regarding the investment opportunities of the firm, and

(b) can capture effective strategic decision making power.

Similarly, it is generally expensive and impractical to call a shareholders' meeting to approve every investment. Consequently, it is necessary to define appropriate organizational mechanisms to identify and implement the long run investment decisions.

Even in the context of financing new investment opportunities it has been observed that

(a) getting approvals, from the appropriate stock market authorities for the flotation of new issues of common stock, involves delays and expenditure, and

(b) the competition would seize the profitable investment opportunities if the firm does not act swiftly.

An outline of this argument can be found in Fazzari and Peterson (1993). As a result the firm may find it necessary to utilize debt instruments to finance capital investments. In other words, the portfolio diversification strategy is an equally important long run decision.

In general, the choice of the debt equity ratio affects the cost of financing investments as well as the degree of control the shareholders can exercise. Firstly, following Marris (1964,p.8) and Vickers (1987,pp.63 ff), it should be noted that an increase in the debt equity ratio entails an increase in the market rate of interest. Consequently, there is a more than proportionate increase in the cost of financing new investments as the debt equity ratio increases. Secondly, an increase in the debt equity ratio reduces the control of the outside shareholders. In such a situation, a risk averse management will reduce investments even if profitable opportunities exist. On the other hand, a risk taking management may finance projects which are otherwise marginal. Both these aspects of the control effect tend to reduce the long run performance of the firm below the potential maximum.

In a fundamental sense the choice of the debt equity ratio has implications for the organization of the firm and the loss of control in addition to the cost effect. See, for instance, Williamson (1988). Both these aspects must be considered simultaneously in the process of defining the optimal portfolio diversification.

On the basis of these arguments the present chapter attempts to model two prominent long term strategic decisions of the management, viz.,
(a) the extent and direction of capital investments; in particular, the rate of growth of the capital stock, and
(b) the optimal mix of financial instruments; that is, the capital structure (often represented by the debt equity ratio).

The rest of the chapter is organized as follows. Section 6.2 examines the operation of the implicit contract as the organizational mechanism to coordinate the long term strategic decisions. Section 6.3 examines the constraints on the decision making process of the management. The specification of the managerial preferences is taken up in section 6.4. Since the model nests a variety of patterns of behavior they are clearly identified in section 6.5. Section 6.6 examines the empirical results in detail.

6.2. The Implicit Contract

The business risk, inherent in the fluctuations in the market conditions, is a major determinant of the short run profits of the firm. As owners of the firm the shareholders bear such risks. Consequently, they attempt to control[1] the decisions which affect the market value of the firm. However, in actual practice, they may not have an effective control due to the following reasons:

(a) diffused shareholding and the free rider problems associated with the seperation of ownership and control alluded to by Berle and Means (1932), and

(b) the equity ownership by the managers which dilutes the control of the shareholders (and outside directors on the board) as

---

1. The expression "corporate control" is used to represent different types of phenomena. They range from the general forces that influence the use of corporate resources to control of voting rights and a majority of seats on the corporation's board of directors. The following definitions are representative:
(a) according to Leech and Leahy (1991) control is the power to exercise discretion over major decision making including the choice of the board of directors,
(b) Cubbin and Leech (1983) describe corporate control in terms of securing a simple majority in a shareholder's vote,
(c) Berle and Means (1932,p.69) emphasized the power to select the board of directors as the crucial aspect of corporate control, and
(d) Fama and Jensen (1983) view corporate control to consist of the right to determine the management of the corporate resources - that is, the right to hire, fire and set compensation of the top level management.

pointed out by Leech and Leahy (1991).

Consequently, the shareholders attempt to delegate decision making responsibilities to the management in the form of an implicit contract. That is, they
(a) invest their money in the capital assets of the firm, and
(b) delegate both the strategic and operating decisions to the management.
The understanding is that the management would endeavor to maximize the market value of the firm. In almost all practical situations such decisions cannot be negated by the shareholders. See, for instance, Walter (1963, p.284).

It can be argued that the management would be willing to accept the responsibility for these decisions. In particular, the growth decision can contribute to the attainment of the managerial objectives in the following ways:
(a) as Francis (1980,p.355) pointed out it enables the firm to convert market prospects to profits,
(b) as noted by Filippi and Zanetti (1971,p.147) it can stimulate growth in the productivity of labor and reduce labor union problems,
(c) as Marris (1964,pp.102 and 106) observed successful expansion of assets enables the management to recommend itself to the more lucrative jobs that it creates, and
(d) increased size becomes a deterrent to takeover raids and enhances the job security of the managers. See, for instance, Kamecke (1993).
Hence, as Marris (1964,pp.46 ff) summed it up, growth of capital assets of the firm provides the management income, power, prestige, and job security.

Similarly, the management views the choice of the debt equity ratio from the following perspectives:
(a) Stultz (1990) and Harris and Raviv (1988) argued that a high debt equity ratio reduces the control of the outside directors and provides the management with far greater control rights, and
(b) as Grossman and Hart (1982,pp.108-9) argued, the management

may consider this as a bonding signal since they are precommitting themselves to generating an adequate cashflow to meet the increased interest bill.
Consequently, the managers choose the debt equity ratio in such a way as to bring their own objectives "into line with those of the shareholders because of the effect on market value. In other words, the management bonds itself to act in the shareholders' interest".

However, it is unrealistic to expect the managers to feel compelled to honor implicit contracts and forego opportunistic wealth acquisition. Instead, having gained some control the management would be prone to diverting resources away from value maximization. See, for instance, Benston (1985).

To reduce this moral hazard on the part of the management the board of directors attempt to discipline them by imposing certain restrictions. The most prominent among such choices is the dividends per share. For, the shareholders may not consider it to be in their interest to accept the postponement of dividend payments for a long time if the expected profits and the capital gains from the investments are uncertain. Similarly, it would be necessary for the shareholders to identify and implement suitable incentive schemes (salaries and other compensation policies) which encourage the management to choose effort levels and attitudes towards risk in line with their objectives. For, the managers will not make efficient decisions if they do not feel sufficiently compensated.

The shareholders may consider reneging to be possible despite these arrangements because further alignment would impose excessive monitoring and bonding costs. See, for instance, Jensen and Meckling (1976), and Garvey and Gaston (1991). That is, some amount of adverse selection and/or moral hazard remains. The shareholders will have to accept some reduction in the market value in order to ensure that the implicit contract is sustainable at an efficient level albeit a second best[2]. See, for instance, Hill and Jones (1992,pp.134 ff).

However, an explicit characterization of the managerial preferences remained elusive. As Yarrow (1976,p.267) put it, "once managerial discretion is allowed, economic theory can have little to say about the components and shapes of managerial utility functions." This has lead Jensen and Warner (1988,p.3) to remark that " understanding the behavior of the corporate organization requires deeper knowledge of its governance and the factors that determine the distribution of power among the corporate managers, shareholders, and directors." Yarrow (1976,p.267) suggested that the "best that can be done is to hypothesize a particular type of objective function, explore its consequences, and where possible, test (the consequences of) the model against the evidence."[3]

Against this backdrop the present chapter attempts to reformulate the capital structure and corporate control hypotheses from the underlying economic theory.

6.3. The Constraints on the Management

Almost all the theoretical models of managerial preferences assume that the management endeavors to maintain the operations of the firm at a level where they can preserve the autonomy of the team by minimizing the interference from the board of directors and/or the shareholders. In their turn, the board of directors can be

---

2. To keep the theoretical as well as the empirical work within manageable limits it will be assumed that the short term operating decisions with respect to the utilization of capital assets are invariably
(a) delegated to the management, and
(b) efficiently chosen by the management.

3. Almost all the empirical studies of the Marris (1964) model, as surveyed in Nyman and Silberston (1978), negated it. Also see the more recent work of Cubbin and Leech (1986).

expected to have adequate information regarding the effect of market conditions and managerial decisions on the market value of the firm. Hence, the management takes into account the implications of their decisions for the market value of the firm. In other words, the valuation frontier (i.e., the relationship between the market value of the firm and the strategic choices - viz., the growth of capital and the debt equity ratio) is one of the effective constraints on managerial decisions. In general, combining the Marris (1964,ch.4) hypothesis with that of Grossman and Hart (1982), the valuation frontier can be represented by

$V = V(g,\theta,X)$

where V = market value of the firm's assets, g = rate of growth of capital assets, θ = debt equity ratio, and X = a vector of variables (to be specified in detail in section 3.2) which have an effect on the market value of the firm.

Marris (1964,ch.4) acknowledged the influence of the following factors on the market value of the firm:

(a) the growth of market demand for the products of the firm resulting from its expansion policy, and

(b) the constraints on the supply of finances and/or the costs of doing business implied by the debt equity ratio.

Consider the relationship between g and V. When the firm is in its early stages there will be an expectation that

(a) many profitable opportunities exist,

(b) an increase in the market share can be achieved through growth by diversification,

(c) there is a positive organizational response due to the increase in the opportunities for recruiting new managers, and

(d) the financial constraints are not yet binding.

See, for example, Heal and Silberston (1972,p.138).

In general, as Marris (1964,pp.116-7) put it, low rates of growth have an efficiency inducing effect which increases the market value of the firm. However, after a certain rate of growth of capital assets there are several adverse effects on the firm. In particular,

(a) on the demand side it is apparent that there are limits on the extent to which the firm can sell more goods while preserving at least a constant rate of profit. See Marris (1971,pp.6 ff).

(b) The progressive shifting of the demand curve cannot be achieved without incurring ever increasing marketing expenditures. It should be generally expected that there are diminishing returns to such expenditure as the ratio of these expenditures to current sales increases. Marris (1971,pp.6 ff) acknowleged this aspect as well.

(c) Marris (1964,pp.114-5) argued that the growth of capital assets and expansion of the level of production are crucially constrained by the availability of competent managerial personnel who can

(i) identify new talent for recruitment,

(ii) reorganize the patterns of delegation, and

(iii) train the new workforce.

Consequently, the market value of the firm can be expected to increase at lower levels of g, reach a maximum and decrease thereafter.

The influence of an increase in the debt equity ratio on the market value of the firm can be examined in the following manner.

(a) In the early stages of growth the firm has many potentially value increasing investments while

(i) the internally generated finances are inadequate to take advantage of these opportunities, and

(ii) there are delays and costs associated with the flotation of new issues.

Borrowing from the external sources increases the market value of the firm though the debt equity ratio increases. This may be called the market effect.

(b) One of the consequences of the increase in the debt equity ratio is the recognition by the lenders that there is a reduction in the margin of assets covering their loan. If they feel that this can give rise to the possibility of the firm being unable to compensate them adequately when the product markets are unfavorable they may sell the shares and consequently reduce the share prices and the market value of the firm. This is the asset effect. See, for instance, Marris (1964,p.8).

(c) The cost effect of leverage is to increase the risk of insolvency for any given probability distribution of earnings. Consequently, the market value of the firm will decline.

In general, at lower levels of the debt equity ratio, the market effect may outweigh the net effect of the others. This tends to increase the market value of the firm. However, the other three effects are likely to overshadow the market effect when the debt equity ratio crosses a certain threshold. Hence, as in the case with increases in g, the relationship between the market value of the firm and the debt equity ratio is also of the inverted U-shape.

One further aspect should be considered. Suppose the debt equity ratio increases for a given volume of investment. Grossman and Hart (1982,pp.108-9), Stultz (1990), and Harris and Raviv (1991, pp.306 ff) argued that due to the decrease in the profit potential the management would be under pressure to maintain the maximum possible efficiency to ensure survival of the management team. In other words, there will be an increase in the productivity of resource use due to an improvement in the efficiency of the management. This is the bonding effect which tends to increase the market value of the firm. That is, the effect of a unit increase in the rate of growth of capital assets on the market value of the firm depends on the debt equity ratio so that

$$V = a_0 - a_1^* g,$$

$$a_1^* = a_1 g - a_2 \theta$$

where $a_2 > 0$ indicates a bonding effect. Hence, in general, the interaction term $g\theta$ will occur in the V equation with a positive sign if the bonding effect is the stronger and with a negative sign if the cost effect is predominant.

Consider a change in any market related variable (X). Assume, for instance, that there is a large unexpected reduction in the demand for the products of the firm. Three possible responses can be conceptualized:

(a) The reduction in the market demand is expected to be of a long term nature and it is possible to adjust the growth of capital assets without any significant cost. In such a case the change in X can be fully accommodated by reducing g. The effect of a unit change in g on the market value of the firm depends only on the value of g.
(b) The reduction in the market demand is expected to be temporary but some reduction in g is considered prudent. Some orders for capital equipment, which can be cancelled without incurring any significant cost, will be withdrawn. However, some capital equipment will remain underutilized at least over the short run. Consequently, the effect of a unit reduction in g on the market value of the firm would still depend on X.
(c) In some cases it is very expensive and impractical to make any changes in g in the short run. In such a situation the market value of the firm will be affected by the entire change in X whatever may be the value of g.
Hence, the effect of a unit change in g on the market valuation can be represented by

$$a_1^* = a_1 g + a_2 X$$

$$V = a_0 + a_1^* g + a_3 Z$$

$$= a_0 + a_1 g^2 + a_2 gX + a_3 Z$$

where all the variables which are very expensive to accommodate have been reclassified as Z. Clearly, a_2 and/or a_3 may be zero in actual practice.

One further observation is in order. As reported in Rastogi and Rao (1995), it appears that only one of the strategic decisions may be delegated to the management. For example, a competitive product range of the firm may indicate that the marketing managers have the best information regarding new avenues for investment and growth of capital assets of the firm. However, if the capital structure decision is delegated to the management, power seeking managers may commit the firm to greater financial risks. The board of directors may then decide to regain control with respect to the capital structure decision. Consequently, even if the management is choosing the capital structure they may not go to the extent of maximizing control they can achieve. Instead, they may operate on the increasing portion of the valuation frontier when plotted against θ. In such cases either θ or θ^2 may have the role of a Z variable. This can also be viewed as a strong bonding effect.

6.4. Managerial Preferences

The maintained hypothesis in all the managerial theories of the firm is that the management associates a positive value with increases in g and θ. For, they increase the prestige and the controlling power of the management over the decision making process of the firm. That is, it is generally postulated that the decision makers would tradeoff market value of the firm to gain control. Formally the preference function[4] can be written as

$$U = V + \lambda_{11}g + \lambda_{21}\theta$$

where $\lambda_{11}, \lambda_{21} > 0$.

However, it can be expected that the viability of the team depends on the changes in the external environment, viz.,
(a) the fluctuations in the product market conditions,

---

4. The hypothesis is however contested. Francis (1980, p.355) argued that " although managers are clearly interested in growth as well as profitability their decision to pursue the objective of the growth of the firm is because of the profit it yields rather than the personal satisfactions obtained from the firm itself getting bigger."

(b) the constraints imposed in the form of dividend payments[5], and
(c) the incentives offered by the board of directors.
Consequently, there is an expectation that the preferences with respect to the strategic choices, will be adapted to these contingencies appropriately.

If these measures succeed in aligning the decision maker's objectives with those of the shareholders it can be expected that there would be a reduction in the extent of tradeoff between the market value of the firm and personal goals like power and prestige. This weak bonding effect adds to the productivity increasing effect alluded to in section 2.2.

Consequently, an appropriate specification of preferences turns out to be

$U = V + \lambda_1^* g + \lambda_2^* \theta$, where

---

5. The general argument is as follows:
(a) The shareholders expect a fair risk adjusted rate of return. Hence, they influence the dividend decisions, and
(b) the management adjusts the capital structure decision keeping this constraint in perspective.
See, for instance, Fisher _et al_ (1989), Koutsoyiannis (1978), Green and Talmor (1986), Friend and Lang (1988), Chang (1992), Ravid and Sudit (1994), and Bardsley (1995). However, it has also been suggested quite often that the shareholders take the capital structure decision into account while fixing the rate of dividends. Copeland and Weston (1988, pp. 569-70) details the argument. The empirical experiences in the Indian context generally support this viewpoint. See, for example, Rao and Sharma (1984), and Balasubramanian (1993). Diametrically opposed to this Harris and Raviv (1990, p.322) argue that the capital structure decision is generally made by the shareholders. Given this, Grabowski and Mueller (1972, p.10) and Rozeff (1982) argue that the dividend and growth of capital decisions are delegated to the management. This study will not examine this alternative formulation.

$\lambda_1^* = \lambda_{11} + \lambda_{12}Y$, and

$\lambda_2^* = \lambda_{21} + \lambda_{22}Y$

This formulation assumes that λ_1^* and λ_2^* represent the extent of the tradeoff between the value of the firm and a unit increase in g and θ respectively. In general, it can be expected that λ_{12}, $\lambda_{22} < 0$ if there is a bonding effect.

Note that the bonding effect has two components as represented in Fig. 6.1[6] :

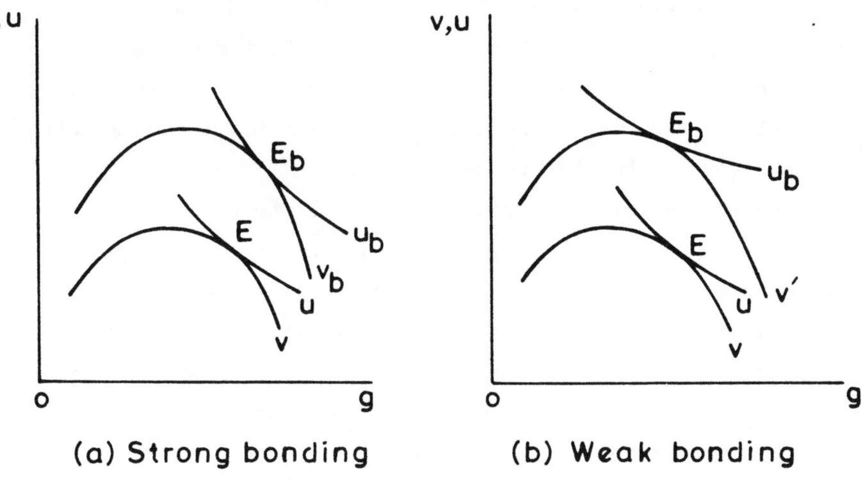

FIG. 6.1. BONDING EFFECTS

6. In this diagram V_1, U_1, and E_1 represent respectively the initial valuation frontier, the preference function, and the optimal choice of g. The valuation frontier shifts to U_b in panel (a) due to the productivity effect. The equilibrium choice of g shifts to E_b. In contrast, in panel (b) the weak bonding effect makes the preference function flatter as portrayed by U_b and the new equilibrium choice of g is E_b.

(a) the productivity effect which shifts the valuation frontier upwards, and

(b) the flattening of the indifference map, representing the managerial preferences.

These are the strong and weak bonding effects respectively.

In practice, either one of these or both the effects may operate.

6.5. Expected Patterns

The empirically expected patterns can now be detailed as follows:

(a) Good market prospects and the flexibility of the constraints may enable the decision makers to pursue the objectives of growth and maintaining corporate control even with a high debt equity ratio. Both the g^2 and θ^2 variables will appear in the valuation function with a negative sign. Similarly, g and θ will appear with positives signs in the preference function.

(b) Suppose the market prospects are good and there is a preference for growth. The management may consider the financial risk to be disproportionate to the gains in corporate control. Growth will be restricted in such a way that the choice of θ is in the increasing portion of the valuation frontier. In other words, the strong bonding effect will be exhibited by the positive sign on θ^2 in the valuation frontier.

(c) There are situations in which the current cashflows are low and financing even the limited growth prospects necessitates debt financing. In such cases there can be a positive preference for θ even if the choice of g is on the increasing portion of the valuation frontier.

(d) On occasions the market prospects may not be encouraging and the cost implications of a high debt equity ratio may be a deterrent for further expansion of the capital assets. Under these conditions both the choices of g and θ will be on the increasing portion of the valuation frontier. It would not be possible to estimate the valuation frontier and the preference function independently. The estimated V function can only represent the expansion path. In addition, the sources of market valuation of assets and the weak bonding effects on managerial preferences will have to be judged from the X and Y variables which remain in the estimated equations.

6.6. Empirical Experience

The information provided in Table 6.1 does not indicate any systematic variation regarding the growth of capital assets in the case of Glaxo. The results for the other firms suggest that GRTH is a result of three factors in several cases:
(a) an improvement in the markets for the products of the firm as reflected by NSAL,
(b) the greater availability of internal finances whenever there is an increase in NPRO and/or a reduction in the pressure to pay dividends, and
(c) an increase in FIRI and the corresponding reduction in the cashflow deter the management from opting for higher growth.
The other prominent results are as follows:
(a) WASA, as an incentive mechanism to deter managerial discretion has been useful in only a few cases,
(b) the market risks reflected by BSRI and INSA do not have a major influence on GRTH, and
(c) TAXT rarely has any influence on GRTH.
On the whole, it can be claimed that the GRTH decision is mostly conditioned by the long term fundamental strengths of the firm such as the product market and internal sources of finances.

Referring to Table 6.2 the capital structure choice exhibits the following patterns.
(a) TAXT has a major influence on DEBT for a majority of the firms. In particular, debt financing is reduced whenever high corporate tax reduces the cashflow and makes the pursuit of a high debt equity ratio undesirable. This is in consonance with the pecking order theory of Myers (1984).
(b) WASA does serve the useful role of making the management bond with the shareholders. The management realizes that an increase in the wages and salaries are a drain on the net cashflows since they are fixed. Consequently, they will restrain themselves from creating a greater interest burden by reducing the debt equity

ratio.

(c) Fluctuations in the product market conditions is the other important influence on DEBT. A ceteris paribus increase in business risk results in (i) an uncertainty in the cashflows and a temporary shortage of internal finances, and (ii) a necessity for larger precautionary inventories and/or an inability to sell the goods produced (as represented by INSA).

(d) The deterrent effect of DIND on DEBT is felt only in the case of a few firms whose cashflows are relatively more volatile.

(e) The market conditions, as reflected in NSAL and NPRO have an influence on DEBT in a few cases.

In general, in their choice of DEBT, the management of most of the firms exhibit a sensitivity to the cashflows of the firm and the costs associated with the operating decisions.

Consider the estimated valuation frontier. From Table 6.3 it should be noted that the managers of 18 firms in the sample have a preference for GRTH. The following observations are pertinent.

(a) Eight firms out of this group operate on the increasing portion of the valuation frontier in their choice of DEBT. This can be inferred from the appearence of DEBT and/or DEBB in the MAVA equation. There is a risk aversion on the part of the management. It is equally appropriate to claim that the managers of these firms exhibit strong bonding effects in the sense of Grossman and Hart (1982). In general, the bonding effects of the choice of WASA operate only through the management's choice of the capital structure. For, this variable does not appear in the estimated MAVA equations with the expected signs. However, in the case of four firms DIND has an independent bonding effect. Dividend constraints are the more effective method of reducing managerial discretion.

(b) The shareholder valuation of the GRTH of capital assets is conditioned by market demand in the context of fourteen of these firms as reflected by the appearence of GNSAL or NSAL in the valuation frontier. The appearance of GNPRO or NPRO for nine firms suggests that the shareholders value NPRO in addition to NSAL while evaluating the GRTH decisions of the management. As a result either the product market conditions and/or the availability of free cashflow almost always dictated the GRTH decision of the management since they had a conditioning role in determining the market value of the firm.

(c) Market risks, as reflected in BSRI, were themselves not an important determinant of MAVA. In other words, so long as there is an increase in the expected level of sales and profits the management is not deterred by market risks.

(d) The interest burden associated with the choice of capital structure had an adverse effect on the market value of the firm in only five cases. Since there is no explicit preference for DEBT it can only be inferred that they exhibited a tendency to over expand though the financial constraints were severe.

(e) The corporate tax policies and liquidity constraints on working capital had an effect on MAVA only in the case of four firms. The claims of the corporate sector about their deterrent effects are exaggerated.

Consider the estimated preference functions in Table 6.4. The following aspects should be noted.

(a) GWASA appears only in the case of Herdillia. In general, it can be argued that the management cannot be restricted in their choice of GRTH by providing them such incentives.

(b) However, the managements of as many as six firms feel restrained by the dividend requirements. This suggests the occurence of a weak bonding effect in an implicit contract. It may be concluded that dividend restricions are a more potent control mechanism for aligning managerial objectives with those of the shareholders.

Table 6.5 indicates that the managements of only five firms have a preference for acquiring corporate control through DEBT. The results for these firms indicate the following salient features.

(a) The market conditions are the major determinant of the market value of the firm since GNSAL or NSAL appear in the MAVA equation for three of these firms.

(b) Two firms have GNPRO or NPRO in the MAVA equation. That is, the shareholders, of even the firms whose managements prefer corporate control, evaluate the performance of the firms in terms of NSAL and/or NPRO.

(c) The risk variables BSRI and FIRI do not have a major influence. It is perhaps most appropriate to conclude that these firms

(i) emphasize stability of the market share and the long term prospects of the firm,

(ii) resort to debt financing due to the shortage of internal sources of finances, and

(iii) limit GRTH due to risk aversion and/or the requirements of bonding expected by the shareholders.

Turning to Table 6.6 it should be noted that the managerial preferences are conditioned by cost considerations. Weak bonding effects are a result of cost factors. Dividend constraints have no effect on the decisions of such firms. The basic reason may be that the risk averse attitude of the management will not induce them to express a preference for DEBT unless their valuation of the market conditions is favorable.

The four firms, whose estimated MAVA equations are presented in Table 6.7 do not provide any evidence of managerial preference for GRTH or DEBT. Hence, the estimated equations represent only the expansion path and not the valuation frontier. The following observations about these firms are pertinent.

(a) Their growth policies are market driven. This is evident from the appearence of NSAL in three cases. Perhaps the market expectations are high enough so that BSRI itself does not have any significant effect on the observed market value of these firms.

(b) There is a paucity of internal finances to undertake the desired expansion of capital assets. NPRO appears only once. Short term operational problems may be the major difficulty. However, the financial risks are not serious enough even when they resort to debt financing. FIRI was significant in only one case.

(c) The operational problems and short term financial constraints (represented by the significance of LIQD and TAXT) make it necessary to provide more than adequate incentives to maintain the desired level of production. For, whenever WASA was in the MAVA equation it has a negative sign.

(d) DIND constraints generate the desired bonding effect in only one case. However, the bonding effect of the the capital structure choice are evident. In fact, DEBT or DEBB appear in three of these cases.

In general, it can be inferred that the management teams of these firms are highly risk averse.

The following general conclusions emerge from this analysis.

(a) The Marris (1964) hypothesis is valid for several firms. The management generally pursues the growth objective at the cost of maximizing the market value of the firm.

(b) The strong bonding effects, as suggested by the Grossman and Hart (1982) hypothesis, occur only in the context of some firms. However, the weak bonding effects are somewhat more frequent.

(c) The managers prefer internal financial sources to finance the growth of the capital assets of the firm. Hence, dividend constraints are far more effective in achieving such bonding when compared to incentive payments.

(d) A growth oriented management generally takes the product market conditions and the internal sources of finance into account while choosing GRTH. They avoid excessive DEBT due to their aversion to increasing the cost of conducting business. This is necessitated by the shareholders' sensitivity to profit generated in addition to the product market conditions.

(e) The possibility of the management pursuing high debt equity ratios to gain corporate control occurs only when the expectations about the external market conditions are favorable and internal finances are not adequate. Even in such cases the management is risk averse in so far as they are sensitive to the high costs of debt financing. For, as employees their gains from taking risks are low while they lose substantially in case of failure. There is no significant evidence of the management seeking or gaining corporate control even when a preference for DEBT is exhibited.

Table 6.1. The GRTH Equation

S.No	Firm	CONS	BSRI	FIRI	NSAL	NPRO
1.	ALB	0.84	-	-	1414.80	-
		(19.84)			(761.70)	
2.	ALEM	39.65	-	-518.72	-	-
		(14.05)		(244.40)		
3.	ARL	3.51	-	-	2477.30	-
		(7.47)			(783.07)	
4.	BASF	22.32	-50.41	-	-	-
		(8.50)	(39.44)			
5.	BAYER	2.08	-	-	-	2.39
		(3.87)				(0.78)
6.	BOOTS	7.12	-	-	0.12	-
		(4.31)			(0.099)	
7.	BORAX	25.54	-	-	-	58.00
		(25.50)				(25.58)
8.	COCHIN	1.93	-	-	21.41	-
		(8.54)			(11.66)	
9.	COLOR	29.08	-	-539.20	-	5.36
		(10.01)		(242.12)		(2.01)
10.	CORO	64.83	-	-	-	-
		(34.81)				
11.	DCW	3.97	-	-	120.22	-
		(4.26)			(41.85)	
12.	DHM	46.50	-	-	-	-
		(20.57)				
13.	DYES	30.50	-40.78	-	-	1.13
		(8.09)	(14.30)			(0.48)
15.	GUJ	1.77	-	-	45.48	-
		(4.01)			(12.24)	
16.	HERDIL	15.02	-	-	0.13	-
		(9.77)			(0.053)	
17.	IDL	25.90	-	-441.06	-	-
		(3.11)		(82.91)		

Table 6.1 (contd.)

18.	JLM	1.96	-	-	893.29	-
		(4.48)			(423.31)	
19.	KANOR	24.66	-	-293.67	-	-
		(8.85)		(155.84)		
20.	NOCIL	5.21	-	-	56.41	-
		(4.78)			(36.39)	
21.	POLY	2.53	-	-	0.076	-
		(3.91)			(0.029)	
22.	RALLIS	34.30	-	-723.47	-	-
		(14.22)		(489.07)		
23.	SANDOZ	64.11	-	-569.25	0.075	-
		(18.19)		(170.03)	(0.039)	
24.	SYNTH	-1.30	-	-	-	1.24
		(2.80)				(0.89)
25.	TATA	43.16	-	-	-	1.05
		(13.70)				(0.27)
26.	UNICHM	10.78	-	-	-	-
		(4.74)				
27.	UNION	-3.23	-	-	-	1.12
		(3.13)				(0.43)

Notes: (1) There was no meaningful explanation for the GRTH choice of GLAXO.

(2) The numbers in the brackets are the standard errors.

(3) The R^2 is corrected for degrees of freedom.

Table 6.1 (contd.)

INSA	TAXT	WASA	DIND	R^2
-90.20	-	-	-	0.15
(83.10)				
-	-32.50			0.45
	(13.42)			
-	-	-	-	0.45
-	-	-	-	0.35
-	-	-	-	0.50
-	-	-	-	0.43
-	-	-	-4.00	0.15
			(2.92)	
-	-	-	-	0.24
-	-	-	-	0.57
-258.14	-	-	-	0.11
(155.06)				
-	-	-	-	0.47
-	-	-156.42	-1.66	0.59
		(104.72)	(1.20)	
-	-	-217.93	-	0.43
		(60.36)		
-	-	-	-	0.56
-	-	-226.28	-	0.31
		(101.59)		
-	-	-	-	0.95

Table 6.1 (contd.)

-	-	-	-7.00	0.17
			(4.63)	
-	-	-	-	0.51
-	-	-	-0.71	0.12
			(0.56)	
-	-	-	-	0.43
-	-	-	-	0.55
-	-	-	-32.72	0.48
			(11.25)	
-	-	-	-	0.05
-	-	-	-18.24	0.78
			(7.94)	
-	-	-	-0.24	0.16
			(0.16)	
-	-	-	-	0.24

Table 6.2. The DEBT Equation

S.No	Firm	CONS	BSRI	NSAL	NPRO	INSA	LIQD
1.	ALB	0.46	-	-	-0.13	-	-
		(0.053)			(0.051)		
2.	ALEM	1.38	2.35	-	-	-	-
		(0.22)	(0.70)				
3.	ARL	1.56	-	-	-	-2.40	-
		(0.47)				(1.22)	
4.	BASF	2.26	-	-	-	-	-
		(0.50)					
5.	BAYER	0.90	1.76	-	-	-	-
		(0.27)	(0.88)				
6.	BOOTS	1.41	-	-	-	-	-
		(0.35)					
7.	BORAX	0.73	-	-	-	-	-
		(0.19)					
8.	COCHIN	9.19	6.09	-	-	-	-
		(2.18)	(1.50)				
9.	COLOR	2.28	-	-	-	-4.02	-
		(0.34)				(1.01)	
10.	CORO	4.49	-	-7.31	-	-	-
		(0.57)		(2.68)			
11.	DCW	2.06	-	-	-	-	-
		(0.34)					
12.	DHM	2.51	-	-	-	-	-
		(0.44)					
13.	DYES	0.79	-	0.0066	-	-	-
		(0.18)		(0.00070)			
14.	GLAXO	0.74	-	-	-	-	-
		(0.15)					
15.	GUJ	2.94	-	-	-	-	-
		(0.39)					
16.	HERDIL	1.58	-	-	-	-1.17	-
		(0.20)				(0.67)	

Table 6.2 (contd.)

17.	IDL	0.45	-	-	-	-	-
		(0.05)					
18.	JLM	1.57	1.05	-	-	-	-0.97
		(0.54)	(0.35)				(0.45)
19.	KANOR	2.25	-	-	-	-	-
		(0.34)					
20.	NOCIL	0.65	4.51	-	-	-	-
		(0.41)	(1.30)				
21.	POLY	0.54	1.88	-	-	-	-
		(0.21)	(0.52)				
22.	RALLIS	1.00	-	-	-	-	-
		(0.19)					
23.	SANDOZ	0.47	-	-	-	-	-
		(0.13)					
24.	SYNTH	0.65	-	-	-	-	-
		(0.28)					
25.	TATA	2.47	-	-	-	-	-
		(0.48)					
26.	UNICHM	1.29	-	-	-	-1.95	-
		(0.21)				(0.48)	
27.	UNION	0.16	0.88	-	-	-	-
		(0.092)	(0.67)				

Table 6.2 (contd.)

TAXT	WASA	DIND	R^2
-0.43	-	-	0.82
(0.13)			
-1.10	-5.79	-	0.84
(0.27)	(1.31)		
-	-	-	0.49
-2.05	-6.34	-	0.66
(0.55)	(2.19)		
-1.89	-	-	0.82
(0.35)			
-	-4.59	-	0.83
	(1.41)		
-0.50	-3.98	-	0.50
(0.25)	(2.50)		
-13.28	-518.85	-	0.74
(3.52)	(183.46)		
-2.02	-	-	0.80
(0.45)			
-2.91	-	-1.02	0.79
(1.07)		(0.30)	
-	-8.62	-	0.73
	(2.10)		
-	-16.54	-	0.72
	(3.36)		
-	-	-0.046	0.93
		(0.013)	
-1.06	-	-	0.66
(0.30)			
-2.29	-	-0.064	0.79
(0.68)		(0.018)	
-1.22	-	-0.26	0.85
(0.32)		(0.081)	

Table 6.2 (contd.)

-0.55	-	-	0.86
(0.12)			
-0.76	-	-	0.89
(0.22)			
-1.20	-6.27	-	0.90
(0.54)	(2.09)		
-	-	-0.030	0.72
		(0.013)	
-1.05	-	-	0.78
(0.40)			
-1.36	-	-	0.64
(0.49)			
-	-1.20	-	0.70
	(0.73)		
-	-3.54	-	0.25
	(2.09)		
-	-13.99	-	0.73
	(3.68)		
-0.35	-2.60	-	0.89
(0.17)	(1.02)		
-	-	-	0.54

Table 6.3. MAVA (GRTH) Equation

S.No	Firm	CONS	GRTT	NSAL	NPRO	GNSAL
1.	ALB	0.81	-0.0029	-	-	0.0083
		(0.65)	(0.0013)			(0.0036)
2.	ARL	0.82	-0.0019	-	-	0.0094
		(0.38)	(0.00027)			(0.0014)
3.	BAYER	3.49	-0.12	0.14	0.59	-
		(3.21)	(0.016)	(0.056)	(0.074)	
4.	BOOTS	10.30	-0.54	-	-	0.13
		(11.80)	(0.036)			(0.0088)
5.	BORAX	1.36	-0.0016	-	-	-
		(0.62)	(0.00047)			
6.	COCHIN	-82.40	-0.19	-	1.33	0.0083
		(13.30)	(0.033)		(0.54)	(0.0014)
7.	COLOR	-24.90	-0.017	-	-	-
		(6.99)	(0.0092)			
8.	DCW	-12.70	-0.031	-	2.91	0.0075
		(5.51)	(0.0061)		(0.60)	(0.0015)
9.	GUJ	-1.10	-0.38	-	-	0.034
		(11.50)	(0.019)			(0.0017)
10.	HERDIL	12.10	-0.043	-	-	0.011
		(1.03)	(0.0054)			(0.0014)
11.	IDL	5.26	-0.0069	0.21	-	-
		(2.45)	(0.0027)	(0.047)		
12.	JLM	0.87	-0.0044	-	1.30	-0.0078
		(0.14)	(0.0042)		(0.49)	(0.0011)
13.	KANOR	2.35	-0.016	0.19	-	-
		(1.79)	(0.0045)	(0.026)		
14.	NOCIL	17.90	-0.16	-	2.50	0.018
		(8.73)	(0.035)		(0.53)	(0.0029)
15.	POLY	10.30	-0.18	-	1.07	0.027
		(3.27)	(0.019)		(0.65)	(0.0029)
16.	RALLIS	-221.00	-0.059	-	5.23	-
		(73.30)	(0.020)		(1.58)	

17.	TATA	65.40	-0.21	-	-	-
		(11.10)	(0.011)			
18.	UNICHM	13.70	-0.015	-	-	-
		(2.77)	(0.0083)			

Note: The interaction terms in the table are

GRTT - $GRTH^2$

DEBB - $DEBT^2$

GNSAL - GRTHxNSAL

GNPRO - GRTHxNPRO

GFIRI - GRTHxFIRI

Table 6.3 (contd.)

GNPRO	GINSA	BSRI	FIRI	GFIRI	LIQD	TAXT
-	-0.53	-	-	-	-	-
	(0.23)					
-	-	-	-	-	-	-
-	-	-	-	-	-	-
-	-	-39.08	-	-	15.41	-
		(25.41)			(7.11)	
0.19	-	-	-	-	-	-
(0.055)						
-	-	-	-	-	74.49	-
					(10.39)	
0.18	-	-	-	-18.16	-	-
(0.099)				(9.97)		
-	-	-	-	-	9.45	-
					(4.49)	
-	-	-	-	-	-	-
-	-	-	-	-	-	-
-	-	-	-	-6.07	-	-
				(2.38)		
-	-	-	-	-	-	-
-	-	-	-	-9.64	-	-
				(2.65)		
-	-	-	-	-	-	-
-	-	-	-	-	-	-
-	-	-	-	-85.11	279.80	-
				(28.88)	(60.86)	

Table 6.3 (contd.)

0.43	-	-	-905.20	-	-	-
(0.024)			(183.56)			
-	-	-	-	-	-	-5.37
						(2.36)

Table 6.3 (contd)

WASA	DIND	DEBT	DEBB	R^2
-	0.17	4.06	-	0.43
	(0.062)	(1.17)		
-	-	-	-	0.67
-	-	-	-	0.95
-	-	-	-	0.93
-	-	-	-	0.30
-	-	-	0.36	0.99
			(0.048)	
-	3.53	-	-	0.68
	(0.49)			
-	-	-	12.60	0.99
			(0.88)	
-	-	-	6.50	0.95
			(2.23)	
-	-	-	2.23	0.73
			(0.81)	
-	-	-	-	0.79
-	-	-	-	0.81
-	2.32	-	3.54	0.98
	(1.08)		(0.56)	
-	-	-	3.27	0.83
			(1.33)	
-	-	-	-	0.93
-653.90	-	-	-	0.88
(311.70)				

Table 6.3 (contd.)

-	-	-	41.53 (7.35)	0.98
-42.02 (15.54)	-	-	-	0.61

Table 6.4. λ (GRTH) Estimates

S.No	Firm	GRTH	GWASA	GDIND
1.	ALB	0.0049	-	-
		(0.0021)		
2.	ARL	0.013	-	-
		(0.0019)		
3.	BAYER	0.51	-	-
		(0.065)		
4.	BOOTS	7.68	-	-
		(0.51)		
5.	BORAX	0.083	-	-0.013
		(0.025)		(0.0038)
6.	COCHIN	0.75	-	-
		(0.13)		
7.	COLOR	0.98	-	-
		(0.54)		
8.	DCW	0.25	-	-
		(0.049)		
9.	GUJ	1.34	-	-
		(0.067)		
10.	HERDIL	1.30	-19.63	-
		(0.16)	(2.42)	
11.	IDL	0.36	-	-
		(0.14)		
12.	JLM	0.017	-	-0.061
		(0.0024)		(0.0087)
13.	KANOR	0.81	-	-
		(0.22)		
14.	NOCIL	1.63	-	-0.22
		(0.36)		(0.049)
15.	POLY	0.90	-	-
		(0.098)		
16.	RALLIS	4.04	-	-
		(1.37)		

Table 6.4 (contd.)

17.	TATA	17.69	-	-7.48
		(0.99)		(0.42)
18.	UNICHM	0.32	-	-0.0072
		(0.18)		(0.0040)

Note: The interaction terms in the table are

GWASA - GRTHxWASA

GDIND - GRTHxDIND

Table 6.5. MAVA (DEBT) Equation

S.No	Firm	CONS	DEBT	NSAL	NPRO	DNSAL	BSRI
1.	DYES	0.97	-13.82	-	-	0.18	-
		(0.86)	(0.57)			(0.0075)	
2.	GLAXO	-1.07	-242.10	-	11.74	-	-
		(11.70)	(140.10)		(2.90)		
3.	SANDOZ	14.50	-122.40	0.18	-	-	-24.78
		(4.85)	(40.86)	(0.017)			(7.66)
4.	SYNTH	-61.40	-134.10	0.42	-	-	-
		(15.30)	(72.38)	(0.064)			
5.	UNION	-61.80	-588.40	0.32	2.22	-	-
		(17.00)	(250.20)	(0.063)	(0.81)		

Note: The interaction terms in the table are

DEBB - $DEBT^2$

DNSAL - DEBTxNSAL

GRTT - $GRTH^2$

Table 6.5 (contd.)

FIRI	DBSRI	LIQD	TAXT	DIND	GRTT	R^2
-	-	-	-	-	-	0.97
-	-	-	-	-	-	0.50
-149.20 (75.64)	-	-	-	-	-	0.93
-	-	48.97 (11.87)	-12.27 (6.16)	-	-	0.79
-	1020.00 (433.90)	-	-	33.28 (8.83)	0.056 (0.016)	0.76

Table 6.6. λ (DEBT) Estimates

S.No	Firm	DEBT	DWASA	DDIND
1.	DYES	21.84	-	-1.28
		(0.89)		(0.052)
2.	GLAXO	360.10	-	-
		(280.80)		
3.	SANDOZ	115.20	-294.80	-
		(38.44)	(98.37)	
4.	SYNTH	174.10	-949.80	-
		(93.99)	(512.70)	
5.	UNION	185.00	-	-
		(78.65)		

Note: The interaction terms in the table are
DWASA - DEBTxWASA
DDIND - DEBTxDIND

Table 6.7. MAVA (Expansion path) Estimates

S.No	Firm	CONS	NSAL	NPRO	BSRI	FIRI	LIQD
1.	ALEM	8.64	0.088	-	-	-166.53	-
		(2.19)	(0.0082)			(45.37)	
2.	BASF	-2.40	-	5.91	-	-	-
		(1.57)		(0.48)			
3.	CORO	-16.40	0.40	-	-	-	-
		(18.74)	(0.051)				
4.	DHM	26.26	0.27	-	-35.79	-	22.27
		(16.89)	(0.043)		(12.56)		(4.76)

Note: The interaction term in the table is
$DEBB - DEBT^2$

Table 6.7 (contd.)

TAXT	WASA	DIND	DEBT	DEBB	R^2
-3.99	-	-	-	3.44	0.98
(1.92)				(0.40)	
-	-	-	5.01	-	0.92
			(1.80)		
-53.63	-	17.01	10.82		0.94
(21.34)		(6.55)	(3.63)		
-	-419.50	-	-	-	0.95
	(127.21)				

CHAPTER 7

SELLING COSTS AND MARKET SHARE

7.1. The Marketing Decision

In chapter 2 it was acknowledged that most of the firms in the corporate sector adopt decentralized forms of organization and delegate the decision making with respect to the utilization of capital assets to the different levels of management primarily due to information advantages. Within an organizational set up of this nature it would be acknowledged that the marketing manager has the best information regarding the market conditions for the products of the firm. Hence, the marketing manager will be expected to obtain the necessary information regarding the market demand for the various products of the firm and choose the level of output of each of the products so as to maximize the profits of the firm. However, the marketing manager does not have the information about all the costs and will not be in a position to calibrate the contribution of the marketing division to the overall profits of the firm. The general manager will also acknowledge this and makes the marketing manager accountable to the market share rather than the profits generated. As such the fundamental decision delegated to the marketing manager is to target the sales of different products of the firm. In their turn, the marketing managers recognize that the credibility of the market share targets will be undermined if they cannot be defended. Consequently, selling costs will be utilized as another policy instrument to make sure that the targets are fulfilled[1].

---

1. Studies of monopolistic competition generally acknowledge that the selling costs incurred by the firm, and advertising in particular, provide the consumers information regarding the firm's products. See, for instance, Chamberlin (1962, pp.275 ff). The resulting shift in the demand curve for the firm and/or the reduction in the elasticity of demand, as noted in Chamberlin (1962, p.135,140), has an active role in generating larger profits. Comanor and Wilson (1979), and Utton (1982,ch.4) contain

The market uncertainty and the instability of the market share under conditions of monopolistic competition is the other aspect which the marketing manager keeps in perspective. In general, it can be expected that the high levels of sales are associated with greater variability. Hence, there will be a tendency on the part of the marketing manager to target a market share in such a way that the temporal variability can be reduced to a minimum. Selling costs also provide the firm a means by which the variability can be reduced[2]. In other words, targetting a market share and defending it by an appropriate choice of selling costs would be the fundamental decisions of the marketing manager even from this perspective.

From an analytical viewpoint the marketing manager of such a decentralized firm is normally expected to
(a) monitor the market environment,
(b) plan the profitable level of sales keeping the market prospects and the firm level constraints in perspective, and
(c) undertake sales efforts commensurate with these plans.

Within this framework managerial discretion is a result of
(a) information asymmetry,
(b) the managerial preferences regarding the short run and long run profits, and
(c) the managerial attitudes towards the risks involved in attaining their goals.
Two aspects of this managerial discretion should be highlighted.
(a) In general, in the long run interests of the firm, a stable market share would be considered desirable even if it entails a

---

1. (contd)
fairly detailed reviews of this and related issues. However, in the context of decentralized decision making alluded to here the role of the selling costs is fundamentally different.

2. More recently Eckard (1987) has shown that selling costs cannot always reduce the instability of the market share.

reduction in the short run profits of the firm. One of the earliest exponents of this position was Baumol (1959).
(b) Selling costs have the role of defending such market share targets.
However, there are two limitations in the use of the selling costs.
(a) There are diminishing returns to information provided by advertising.
(b) Rival firms react in such a way as to limit the effects of advertising by a given firm.
See, for instance, Chamberlin (1962, p.146) and Netter (1982).
There is a possibility of excessive selling costs[3] if the marketing manager is risk averse.

---

3. There is a persistent suggestion in the monopolistic competition literature that the profit maximizing level of selling costs would be excessive from the perspective of consumer welfare. The Dixit and Norman (1978) viewpoint was that for a given volume of sales, which the firm offers at the pre- or post- advertising level, the market price increases with the level of advertising. Hence, there is a reduction in the welfare since the consumer derives the same level of satisfaction by incurring a higher expenditure. Also see Basu (1993, pp.99 ff). On the other hand, Schmalensee (1978) argued that an increase in advertising deters entry, reduces the elasticity of demand, and the volume of sales which maximize profit. Also see Weiss et al (1983) and Sass and Saurman (1995). Based on this argument it can be shown that the consumer welfare is reduced for two reasons:
(a) for a given volume of sales the reduction in the elasticity of demand reduces consumer welfare given the Spence (1977) formula, and
(b) the reduction in the profit maximizing level of sales reduces the welfare further.
However, both the theoretical and empirical validity of these arguments is contested. Even the discretionary managerial behavior hypothesis of Baumol (1959) points out the possibility of excessive dependence on selling costs to maintain a high market

Stated in very general terms the marketing manager has two basic options when these two decisions are considered together.

(a) Target a high market share which enhances the profit prospects of the firm and choose a sufficiently high level of sales promotion to ensure its attainability.

(b) Set a low target which can be easily achieved and choose an adequately high level of sales promotion so that the general manager can be convinced that higher targets are not attainable.

Both these alternatives suggest the possibility of selling costs being excessive[4].

It should be reiterated that this type of excessive selling costs is not specific to any one form of market structure. Instead, it is a result of the discretionary use of resources by the management in an environment characterized by information asymmetry between the different echelons of the organization. Managerial inefficiencies of this nature are pervasive.

The excessive advertising created by the market structure

3.(contd)

share. The basic difference between this approach and the conventional argument of monopolistic competition is that in this analytical structure consumer welfare is not the reference point for defining selling costs as excessive. However, both these approaches to excessive selling costs have one thing in common. They emphasize the nature of the market conditions, i.e., monopolistic competition or oligopoly, as the primary source. To that extent excessive selling costs are essentially a result of the allocative inefficiency intrinsic to the operation of imperfect product markets.

4. This type of excessive advertising is far more damaging both from the viewpoint of the firm and the consumers of its products. Rao (1989, ch.5) contains the earliest acknowledgement of this aspect of managerial decisions. However, this issue has not received the attention it deserves.

itself is difficult to control. However, the general manager is likely to be in a position to ascertain the impact of the decisions of the marketing manager on the overall profits of the firm. As such it possible to reduce the excessive advertising created by the discretionary use of resources by the management. For, adequate incentives can be provided or constraints can be placed on the marketing manager to achieve compliance[5]. This viewpoint was briefly outlined in Coughlan and Sen (1989).

Against this backdrop the present study
(a) attempts to model the influence of the marketing manager's choice of selling costs on the profits of the firm in the context of decentralized organizations, and
(b) specifies a model of preferences of the marketing manager, and in particular the effects of Y on their choices, on the basis of the underlying economic theory.

The rest of the chapter is organized as follows. Section 7.2 provides the details of the model. The empirical results are outlined in section 7.3.

7.2. The Model

The perception of the general manager, regarding the profit generating potential of the decisions of the marketing manager, is one of the constraints on the market share target and the selling effort. Hence, it is necessary to specify the relationship between profits, volume of sales, and selling costs.

Under conditions of monopolistic competition the demand curve for the firm's products will be
$p = f(S)$; $f_1 < 0$, where
p = price per unit of sales,

---

5. Direct control of decisions will not be in consonance with the decentralized form of organization. It will be utilized as a last resort if the losses due to moral hazard are high and persistent.

S = volume of output and sales, and

f_1 = derivative of f with respect to sales.

Similarly, the cost of conducting the desired volume of sales can be represented by

C = C(S)

This cost is expected to be such that the average cost curve is U-shaped. Hence, the profit function

$\pi = \pi(S)$

has an inverted U-shape.

Consider the relationship between profits and the selling costs. When the level of advertising is low there will be an expectation that

(a) the consumer can benefit from the additional information made available by advertising, to the extent they can economize on their search costs, and therefore reveal a higher demand curve for the firm's products,

(b) the additional revenue generated by the increase in demand would be commensurate with the selling costs and an increase in profits can be achieved.

Hence, initially it can be expected that

$\pi = \pi(S,A)$; $\pi_2 > 0$, where

A = level of selling costs

for any given value of S. However, as A increases there is a reduction in the value of advertising to the consumer. The shifts in the demand curve will decrease monotonically. Surely, for some level of selling costs the increase in sales revenue will not be commensurate with it. That is, it is difficult to maintain the rate of profit generated by the additions to the selling costs. In general, it can be expected that the relationship between π and A is also of the inverted U-shape.

Suppose the marketing manager decides to increase the level of advertising at the current level of sales. It can be argued that this choice will be motivated by the expectation that a larger market share can be generated over time and/or it can be stabilized. In other words, by increasing the selling costs the marketing manager is providing an assurance to the general manager that there will be an improvement in the long run profits of the firm. The credibility of the marketing manager will be eroded if the expected increase in profits does not materialize. Hence, they will be under pressure to increase efficiency and generate the maximum possible profits. Both these aspects represent a positive synergy. This bonding effect can be incorporated in the specification of the profit function by acknowledging that the effect of a unit increase in S depends on A. In particular, $\pi = a_0 - a_1^* S$, where

$$a_1^* = a_1 S - a_2 A$$

In this specification $a_2 > 0$ indicates that the synergy effects outweigh the cost effects. However, $a_2 < 0$ occurs if the cost effect is predominant. In general, introducing the interaction term SA in the profit function is essential.

Several other market related variables will also have an effect on the profits of the firm. Prominent among them are
(a) the market risks indicated by the changes in demand created by factors which are not under the control of the management,
(b) the financial risks reflected by the cost implications of the financial mix for long term and working capital sources, and
(c) the policies of the government with respect to taxation and short term liquidity.

These effects can be of three types.
(a) Consider an unexpected reduction in the market demand caused by an exogenous variable X. If, on their appraisal, the management considers this to be of a long term nature there will be suitable adjustments in the sales targets and/or the level of advertising. The effect of a unit change in X on the profits of the firm depends exclusively on the S and A decisions of the marketing manager. The variations in X will not have any further influence on π.
(b) If the reduction in demand is expected to be of a short term nature the marketing manager will plan some changes in S and A to

adjust to this. However, some of the plans for production and procurement of resources cannot be altered except at a great cost. In particular, there can be large fixed costs of decreasing or increasing these quantities at short notice. Hence, though some short term adjustments are taken up they may not fully neutralize the effect of X. That is, in addition to the effects of S and A, profits will be affected by the changes in X to some extent.

(c) On occasions the effects of the changes in X may be such that the costs of making adjustments in S and/or A will not be commensurate with the expected gains. In such cases, the entire effect of the changes in X on π will be independent of the choices of S and A.

In general, the effect of a unit change in A on the profits of the firm can be written as

$$a_1^* = a_1 A + a_2 X$$

$$\pi = a_0 + a_1^* A + a_3 Z$$

where all the X variables which are very expensive to accommodate are reclassified as Z. The values of a_1, a_2, and a_3 depend on which of the three cases mentioned above materialize. In particular,

(a) $a_3 = 0 = a_2$ if the effect of X can be fully neutralized by managerial decisions,

(b) $a_3 = 0$ if partial adjustments are possible, and

(c) $a_1 = 0 = a_2$ if the adjustments are too expensive from the viewpoint of the management.

A general specification of the profit function emerges from this analysis. Let

(a) C be a (px1) vector of decisions,

(b) X be a (qx1) vector of market related variables, and

(c) Z be a (sx1) vector of variables which cannot be accommodated in the decision making process despite their expected effects on profits.

The profit function will then be of the form

$\pi = A_0 + C'A_1C + C'A_2X + A_3Z$, where

C' is the transpose of C, and A_0, A_1, A_2, and A_3 are matrices of appropriate dimensions.

The specification of the preference function can now proceed as follows. Note that the management can be expected to place a positive value on

(a) the profit π because it offers them job security,
(b) the market share implied by S due to the prestige they associate with a high market share, and
(c) A, the selling costs, since it would be necessary to create and/or defend a desired level of S.

That is, it can be generally postulated that the marketing manager would tradeoff profits to attain the objectives of a high market share in the long run. Formally the preference function can be written as

$U = \pi + \lambda_1^* S + \lambda_2^* A$, where $\lambda_1^*, \lambda_2^* > 0$.

However, it can be expected that the extent of tradeoff can be reduced by the general manager offering incentives and informing the marketing manager of the dividend expectations of the shareholders. Consequently, it can be postulated that the preferences will be adapted to these contingencies appropriately. The meaningful specification of λ_1^* and λ_2^* will therefore be

$\lambda_1^* = \lambda_{11} + \lambda_{12} Y$, and

$\lambda_2^* = \lambda_{21} + \lambda_{22} Y$, where

Y = incentives and constraints.
In general, it is presumed that $\lambda_{11}, \lambda_{21} > 0$, while $\lambda_{12}, \lambda_{22} < 0$.

In the context of the general model the preference function can be specified as follows. Let Y be a (rx1) vector of characteristics representing the constraints and the incentives which the management values. The preference function takes the form

$U = \pi + C'\lambda Y$

The empirically expected patterns can now be detailed as follows.

(a) Good market prospects and the constraints not being binding may enable the management to pursue both the objectives of maintaining a high market share and defensive advertising. Both the S^2 and A^2 variables will then appear in the profit function with a negative sign. Similarly, the S and A variables will appear with positive signs in the preference function.
(b) Suppose the market prospects are good and there is a preference for a high market share. The management may find it unnecessary to undertake any defensive advertising. In such a case the choice of A will be on the increasing portion of the profit function.
(c) There are situations in which the limited market share prospects afforded by the competition necessitate a vigorous defense. In such a case it is possible to observe a positive preference for A even if the choice of S is in the increasing portion of the profit constraint.
(d) On occasions the market prospects may not be encouraging and the management may find both the pursuit of excessive market share and selling costs undesirable or indefensible. Under these conditions both the choices of S and A will be on the increasing portion of the profit curve. In such cases it would be possible to estimate the expansion path alone.

7.3. The Results

The salient features of the empirical results are the following.
(a) The NSAL decision is invariably determined by NFAS. See Table 7.1. This suggests that most of the marketing managers have a target for capacity utilization in perspective. The other major influence is the availability of finances indicated by DEBT and LIQD. The costs associated with the financial mix, reflected by FIRI, is also significant. The management is also sensitive to the DIND requirements defined by the shareholders though their response to incentives in the form of WASA are not significant.
(b) It can be concluded from Table 7.2 that the higher the NSAL the higher the requirement of GNEX. This is reflected by the presence of NFAS for some firms. The shareholders' expectations regarding DIND payments is a fairly effective constraint in curbing

excessive selling expenses. The availability and the cost of finances also places a limit on GNEX. Given the propensity of the management to attempt market share stabilization it is not surprising that a ceteris paribus increase in business risk reflected in BSRI is necessitating a higher GNEX.

(c) The managements of twenty firms in the sample, as Table 7.3 indicates, have a preference for excessive selling expenses. 11 firms out of this group operate on the increasing portion of the NPRO in their choice of NSAL. Further, whenever a high NSAL is chosen the management is sensitive to the need to maintain higher efficiency and generate greater profits. There is a general tendency to choose a low target for market share and try to defend it by excessive advertising. Hence, there is an overwhelming confirmation of the major hypothesis of the present study. Given the sensitivity to profit generated it is reasonable to expect that the management takes the costs of conducting sales, as reflected in DEBT, GDEBT, FIRI, and/or GFIRI in a majority of cases, into account. For 8 firms in the sample the business risks are so significant that they have an important effect on profits whatever may be the selling effort to stabilize the market share.

(d) The estimated preference functions for these firms exhibited in Table 7.4 suggest that the dividend constraints are more effective in reducing managerial discretion. The incentive mechanisms are not equally as effective. In general, as Drucker (1986, p.303) remarked, compensation mechanisms can be notoriously ineffective. At best they can induce inefficient decision making if the payments are inadequate.

(e) Table 7.5 suggests that only five firms in the sample exhibited a preference for excessive NSAL while operating on the increasing portion of NPRO with respect to their choice of GNEX. Perhaps these firms operate in markets with little business risk and/or their market shares are too small to attract competition. However, the managements of even these firms consider it necessary to increase the efficiency in the decision making process whenever DIND is high. Table 7.6 suggests that the managers of such firms need not alter their preferences to changes in WASA or DIND.

(f) Two firms did not exhibit any excess with respect to NSAL or GNEX. See Table 7.7. However, Dyestuffs and Chemicals gains by market expansion and Union Carbide by increasing GNEX. In both the cases excessive per unit costs of conducting a given volume of sales appear to be the major constraint.

The major conclusions from this analysis are as follows.

(a) There is a general tendency on the part of the marketing managers to set a low target of market share and defend it by excessive advertising.

(b) They are generally risk averse and are sensitive to cost changes and dividend requirements. This inhibits the possibility of setting a high market share and defending it by excessive advertising.

(c) Excessive advertising will not be observed only in the case of firms which have a relatively stable and/or low market share given the product market conditions.

Table 7.1. The NSAL Equation

S.No	Firm	Cons	NFAS	BSRI	FIRI	DEBT	LIQD
1.	ALB	0.0065	-	-	-	-	-
		(0.0023)					
2.	ALEM	0.0059	0.0040	-	-	-	-
		(0.0038)	(0.00038)				
3.	ARL	0.00082	0.0018	-	-	-	-
		(0.00032)	(0.00032)				
4.	BASF	0.13	0.0065	-	-	-0.062	-
		(0.039)	(0.00069)			(0.010)	
5.	BAYER	0.013	0.0049	-	-	-0.018	-
		(0.0062)	(0.00028)			(0.0070)	
6.	BOOTS	-0.028	0.0074	-	-	-	0.017
		(0.0085)	(0.00031)				(0.0055)
7.	BORAX	-0.0029	0.0060	-	-	-	-
		(0.0012)	(0.00056)				
8.	COCHIN	0.19	0.0042	-0.25	-	-	-
		(0.063)	(0.00039)	(0.083)			
9.	COLOR	-0.026	0.0025	-	-	-	-
		(0.014)	(0.00028)				
10.	CORO	0.017	0.0016	-	-	-	-
		(0.015)	(0.00018)				
11.	DCW	-0.025	0.0013	-	-1.01	-	0.075
		(0.022)	(0.00014)		(0.31)		(0.020)
12.	DHM	0.0072	0.0043	-	-	-0.022	-
		(0.0023)	(0.00037)			(0.011)	
13.	DYES	-0.038	0.0020	-	-	-	0.19
		(0.090)	(0.00035)				(0.081)
14.	GLAXO	-0.0080	0.0045	-	-	-	-
		(0.011)	(0.00024)				
15.	GUJ	0.14	0.0012	-	-0.98	-	-
		(0.034)	(0.00012)		(0.48)		
16.	HERDIL	0.013	0.0028	-	-	-0.019	-
		(0.057)	(0.00021)			(0.0057)	

Table 7.1 (contd)

17.	IDL	0.010	0.0025	-	-	-	-
		(0.0060)	(0.00023)				
18.	JLM	0.0013	0.016	-	-0.35	-	-
		(0.0032)	(0.0018)		(0.096)		
19.	KANOR	-0.0034	0.0011	-	-0.59	-	0.036
		(0.018)	(0.000061)		(0.17)		(0.016)
20.	NOCIL	-0.23	0.0057	-	-	-0.021	0.083
		(0.063)	(0.00043)			(0.012)	(0.042)
21.	POLY	0.029	0.0024	-	-	-0.020	-
		(0.0070)	(0.00012)			(0.0055)	
22.	RALLIS	0.076	0.0078	-	-	-	-
		(0.014)	(0.00058)				
23.	SANDOZ	-0.067	0.0095	-	-	-0.074	0.059
		(0.025)	(0.00082)			(0.030)	(0.022)
24.	SYNTH	0.014	0.0026	-	-	-0.022	-
		(0.0049)	(0.00029)			(0.0098)	
25.	TATA	0.028	0.00081	-	-	-	-
		(0.0092)	(0.000064)				
26.	UNICHM	-0.074	0.0061	-	-	-	0.065
		(0.040)	(0.00050)				(0.034)
27.	UNION	-0.012	0.0039	-	-	-0.12	0.072
		(0.040)	(0.00093)			(0.033)	(0.014)

Note: Figures in the brackets are the standard errors.

Table 7.1 (contd)

TAXT	WASA	DIND	R^2
-	-	0.00075	0.76
		(0.00033)	
-	-	-	0.95
-0.0026	-	0.00022	0.99
(0.0011)		(0.000039)	
-	0.16	-	0.94
	(0.078)		
-	-	-	0.97
-	-	-	0.99
-	-	-	0.93
-	-	-	0.92
-0.044	-	0.0043	0.98
(0.020)		(0.00071)	
-	-	-	0.92
-0.050	-	0.0013	0.98
(0.015)		(0.00050)	
-	-	-	0.99
-	1.22	0.0045	0.94
	(0.44)	(0.0020)	
-	-	-	0.97
-	-	-	0.90
-	-	-	0.95

Tabe 7.1 (contd)

-0.018	-	-	0.96
(0.010)			
-0.011	0.049	-	0.93
(0.0044)	(0.023)		
-	-	-	0.97
-	-	-	0.96
-	-	-	0.97
-	-	-	0.98
-	-	-	0.95
-	-	-	0.95
-	-	-	0.93
-	-	-	0.95
-0.11	-	-	0.95
(0.039)			

Table 7.2. The GNEX Equation

S.No	Firm	Cons	NFAS	BSRI	FIRI	INSA	DEBT
1.	ALB	0.063	-	-	-	-	-
		(0.0043)					
2.	ALEM	0.54	-	-	-	-	-0.20
		(0.060)					(0.043)
3.	ARL	0.060	0.010	-	-	-	-
		(0.010)	(0.0032)				
4.	BASF	0.15	0.0029	-	-	-	-
		(0.011)	(0.0012)				
5.	BAYER	0.22	-	-	-	-	-
		(0.020)					
6.	BOOTS	0.33	-	-	-2.77	-	-
		(0.048)			(1.36)		
7.	BORAX	0.091	-	0.063	-	-	-0.057
		(0.010)		(0.045)			(0.041)
8.	COCHIN	0.0044	0.000014	-	-	-	-
		(0.00079)	(0.0000053)				
9.	COLOR	0.034	0.00092	-	-	-	-
		(0.0037)	(0.00020)				
10.	CORO	0.095	-	-	-	-	-
		(0.020)					
11.	DCW	0.16	-	-	-	-	-0.039
		(0.012)					(0.012)
12.	DHM	0.062	0.00067	-	-	-	-
		(0.0044)	(0.00014)				
13.	DYES	0.041	-	-	-	0.064	-
		(0.011)				(0.040)	
14.	GLAXO	0.21	-	-	-	-	-0.071
		(0.021)					(0.062)
16.	HERDIL	0.080	0.00069	-	-	-	-
		(0.0075)	(0.00029)				

Table 7.2 (contd)

17.	IDL	0.30	-	-	-1.36	-	-
		(0.031)			(0.54)		
18.	JLM	0.11	-	0.10	-	-	-
		(0.0098)		(0.037)			
19.	KANOR	0.20	-	-	-	0.61	-0.040
		(0.083)				(0.28)	(0.022)
20.	NOCIL	0.078	-	0.14	-	-	-
		(0.014)		(0.037)			
21.	POLY	0.070	0.00037	0.052	-	-	-
		(0.010)	(0.00015)	(0.026)			
22.	RALLIS	0.058	-	-	-	0.17	-
		(0.022)				(0.12)	
23.	SANDOZ	0.38	0.0038	0.19	-	-	-
		(0.045)	(0.0017)	(0.095)			
24.	SYNTH	0.18	0.0019	0.36	-3.23	-	-
		(0.070)	(0.0010)	(0.090)	(1.52)		
25.	TATA	0.076	-	-	-	-	-
		(0.043)					
26.	UNICHM	0.21	-	-	-	-	-0.17
		(0.017)					(0.052)
27.	UNION	0.041	-	-	-	0.19	-
		(0.012)				(0.059)	

Note: There was no meaningful equation for GLAXO.

Table 7.2 (contd)

LIQD	TAXT	WASA	DIND	R^2
-	-	-	-	0.97
-	-	-1.21 (0.29)	-0.0045 (0.0018)	0.98
-	-	-	-	0.82
-	-	-	-	0.97
-	-	-	-0.0029 (0.0011)	0.94
-	-	-	-0.029 (0.017)	0.96
-	-	-	-	0.93
-	-	-	-	0.82
-	-	-	-	0.96
0.027 (0.0072)	-0.16 (0.038)	-	-	0.91
-	-	-	-	0.92
-	-0.020 (0.0082)	-	-	0.99
-	-	-	-	0.96
-	-	-	-	0.88
-	-	-	-0.015 (0.0045)	0.94

Table 7.2 (contd)

-	-	-	-0.039 (0.018)	0.93
-	-	-	-	0.96
-	-	-0.77 (0.38)	-	0.91
-	-	-	-0.00094 (0.00050)	0.91
-	-	-	-	0.92
-	-	-	-	0.96
-	-	-	-0.18 (0.038)	0.97
-	-	-	-0.0074 (0.0032)	0.74
0.14 (0.040)	-	-	-0.089 (0.031)	0.56
-	-	-	-	0.92
-	-	-	-	0.98

Table 7.3. NPRO (GNEX) Equation

S.No	Firm	Cons	GNEXX	NFAS	GNFAS	BSRI	GBSRI
1.	ALB	4.51	-918.30	-	-	-1.32	-
		(0.86)	(214.20)			(0.47)	
2.	ALEM	0.72	-7.01	-0.073	-	-	-
		(0.38)	(4.47)	(0.048)			
3.	ARL	0.55	-115.50	-	2.38	-	-
		(0.065)	(17.31)		(0.36)		
4.	BASF	63.30	-2697.00	-	15.81	-	-
		(9.14)	(380.10)		(2.23)		
5.	BAYER	11.20	-124.80	-	-	-	-
		(2.82)	(36.11)				
6.	BOOTS	3.61	-14.21	-	-	-	-
		(0.77)	(5.09)				
7.	COCHIN	61.40	-2.89*	-	81.34	-	-
		(4.01)	(0.23)		(6.37)		
8.	COLOR	2.86	-2743.00	-	5.04	-	-
		(0.83)	(367.00)		(0.68)		
9.	DCW	16.70	-610.30	-	-	-4.50	-
		(3.42)	(137.20)			(2.21)	
10.	DHM	8.75	-2568.00	-	4.40	-	-
		(3.60)	(1192.00)		(2.04)		
11.	GLAXO	70.40	-1202.00	-	-	-	-
		(24.70)	(590.50)				
12.	HERDIL	4.06	-683.50	-	0.94	-	-
		(0.85)	(172.80)		(0.24)		
13.	IDL	4.33	-94.64	-	-	-	-
		(3.04)	(35.37)				
14.	JLM	-0.81	-26.45	-	-	-	6.10
		(0.18)	(14.33)				(3.31)
15.	KANOR	10.80	-186.90	-	-	1.54	-
		(3.66)	(80.01)			(0.70)	
16.	NOCIL	11.60	-1831.00	-	-	-	497.90
		(5.58)	(932.70)				(253.70)

Table 7.3 (contd)

17.	POLY	27.20	-4717.00	-	3.45	-	488.20
		(3.70)	(811.40)		(0.59)		(83.98)
18.	SANDOZ	1.81	-42.31	-	0.32	-	15.99
		(0.29)	(11.87)		(0.089)		(4.49)
19.	SYNTH	6.92	-123.40	-	0.48	-	88.62
		(1.48)	44.34)		(0.17)		(31.85)
20.	UNICHM	4.78	-84.45	-	-	-	-
		(1.48)	(30.43)				

Note: * The coefficient is 2.89×10^6 and the standard error is 0.23×10^6.

The interaction terms in the table are

GNEXX - $GNEX^2$

GNFAS - GNEX x NFAS

GBSRI - GNEX x BSRI

GFIRI - GNEX x FIRI

GDEBT - GNEX x DEBT

NSALL - $NSAL^2$

Table 7.3 (contd)

FIRI	GFIRI	DEBT	GDEBT	INSA	LIQD	TAXT
-	-	-1.23	-	-	-	-1.25
		(0.38)				(0.38)
-	-	-	-2.84	-	-	-
			(1.81)			
-	-	-	-	-	-	-
-	-	-2.11	-	-	-	-
		(0.49)				
-	-	-	-	-	-	-4.30
						(1.90)
-	-116.80	-	-	-	-	-4.05
	(41.81)					(1.15)
-	-	-1.16	-	-	-	-
		(0.31)				
-	-	-	-	-	-	-
-	-	-	-47.18	-	-	-
			(10.61)			
-	-	-2.55	-	-	-	-1.57
		(0.77)				(0.81)
-	-	-	-169.40	-	-	-7.99
			(83.23)			(3.00)
-	-	-	-	-	-	-
-	-257.00	-12.31	-	-	3.12	-
	(96.04)	(4.61)			(1.38)	
-	-	-	-	0.90	0.80	-0.36
				(0.45)	(0.17)	(0.10)
-49.16	-	-	-12.32	-	-	-1.35
(10.08)			(5.28)			(0.74)
-61.06	-	-	-	-	-	-
(28.17)						

Table 7.3 (contd)

-	-	-4.38	-	-	-	-
		(0.96)				
-	-	-	-	-	-	-
-	-797.60	-	-	-	-	-
	(286.70)					
-29.26	-	-	-28.78	-	-	-
(18.02)			(10.37)			

Table 7.3 (contd)

WASA	DIND	NSAL	NSALL	R^2
-	-	-	0.00090 (0.00041)	0.88
-	-	0.037 (0.012)	-	0.57
-	-	-	-	0.65
-	0.069 (0.036)	-	-	0.80
-25.09 (12.79)	-	-	0.00014 (0.000016)	0.90
-	-	0.050 (0.0032)	-	0.98
-	-	-	-	0.89
-	0.12 (0.37)	-	-	0.90
-	-	-	0.00013 (0.000018)	0.89
-	-	0.025 (0.011)	-	0.82
-32.94 (8.21)	-	-	-	0.82
-	-	0.021 (0.0073)	-	0.77
-	-	-	0.00096 (0.00046)	0.49
-	0.27 (0.043)	-	-	0.93
-	-	0.015 (0.0051)	-	0.84
-	-	0.051 (0.0084)	-	0.84

Table 7.3 (contd)

-	-	-	-	0.60
-	-	-	0.000069 (0.000013)	0.82
-28.80 (11.45)	-	-	-	0.40
-	-	-	-	0.23

Table 7.4. λ (GNEX) Estimates

S.No	Firm	GNEX	GWASA	GDIND
1.	ALB	116.50	-	-1.84
		(27.17)		(0.43)
2.	ALEM	7.56	-17.02	-0.064
		(4.82)	(10.85)	(0.041)
3.	ARL	13.77	-	-
		(2.06)		
4.	BASF	828.10	-	-
		(116.70)		
5.	BAYER	53.92	-	-0.72
		(15.60)		(0.21)
6.	BOOTS	18.82	-29.62	-1.51
		(6.74)	(10.60)	(0.54)
7.	COCHIN	2.53*	-	-
		(1.97)		
8.	COLOR	188.60	-	-
		(25.24)		
9.	DCW	194.80	-	-
		(43.80)		
10.	DHM	270.40	-	-
		(128.40)		
11.	GLAXO	509.80	-	-
		(250.50)		
12.	HERDIL	109.70	-	-20.97
		(27.74)		(5.30)
13.	IDL	57.36	-	-7.31
		(21.44)		(2.73)
14.	JLM	5.52	-	-
		(2.99)		
15.	KANOR	77.09	-	-
		(33.00)		
16.	NOCIL	284.00	-	-3.43
		(144.70)		(1.75)

Table 7.4 (contd)

17.	POLY	657.20	-	-
		(113.00)		
18.	SANDOZ	32.16	-	-15.17
		(9.03)		(4.26)
19.	SYNTH	44.67	-	-1.83
		(16.06)		(0.66)
20.	UNICHM	35.17	-	-
		(12.67)		

Note: The interaction terms in the table are
GWASA - GNEX x WASA
GDIND - GNEX x DIND

Table 7.5. NPRO (NSAL) Equation

S.No	Firm	Cons	NSALL	NNFAS	BSRI	FIRI	NFIRI
1.	BORAX	-0.11	-0.00067	0.0079	-	-	-
		(0.13)	(0.00011)	(0.0013)			
2	CORO	-1.41	-0.00019	0.00053	15.26	-153.20	-
		(3.56)	(0.000092)	(0.00026)	(5.11)	(38.57)	
3.	GUJ	-5.21	-0.000048	0.00012	-	-	-0.094
		(3.56)	(0.0000076)	(0.000018)			(0.015)
4.	RALLIS	-15.50	-0.000023	0.00037	-	-	-
		(5.72)	(0.000011)	(0.00017)			
5.	TATA	-20.40	-0.00017	0.00028	-	-	-
		(4.63)	(0.000035)	(0.000057)			

Note: The interaction terms in the table are

NSALL - $NSAL^2$

NNFAS - NSAL x NFAS

NFIRI - NSAL x FIRI

Table 7.5 (contd)

LIQD	TAXT	DIND	GNEX	R^2
-	-	0.036	-	0.79
		(0.012)		
-	-	-	75.86	0.53
			(28.18)	
-	-21.04	1.33	-	0.88
	(6.18)	(0.17)		
12.86	-	0.17	-	0.86
(5.02)		(0.029)		
11.19	-16.40	11.29	-	0.94
(7.11)	(7.11)	(2.44)		

Table 7.6. λ (NSAL) Estimates

S.No	Firm	NSAL
1.	BORAX	0.0038
		(0.00063)
2.	CORO	0.0089
		(0.0043)
3.	GUJ	0.012
		(0.0019)
4.	RALLIS	0.0035
		(0.0016)
5.	TATA	0.0093
		(0.0019)

Table 7.7. NPRO (EXPANSION PATH) Estimates

S.No	Firm	Cons	GNEX	NSAL	INSA	FIRI	DEBT
1.	DYES	-0.54	-	46.78	8.52	-	-6.76
		(1.27)		(4.27)	(3.87)		(0.60)
2.	UNION	30.90	163.14	-	-	-398.27	-
		(6.06)	(61.99)			(79.05)	

Table 7.7 (contd)

TAXT	WASA	R^2
-	-	0.90
-15.87	-141.50	0.80
(4.42)	(36.36)	

CHAPTER 8

PRODUCTION INVENTORY DECISIONS

8.1. The Focus

The demand curves for the different products offered by diversified modern corporations are subject to two types of randomness.

(a) The market environment in which such firms operate is one of the sources. It has an effect on all the firms in a given market.

(b) The actions and reactions of the rival firms is the other source. Such effects are firm specific.

The management of the firm is expected to alter its production plans in line with the market prospects irrespective of the sources of the demand fluctuations.

Suppose the firm is able to anticipate the changes in demand with some degree of certainty. The management can then envisage either one or a combination of two possible policies.

(a) If production is flexible expost, in the sense that instantaneous and abrupt changes do not entail significant marginal costs, the firm may adjust the workforce, the utilization of existing labor, and/or compensation policies to generate the desired change in production. See, for instance, Aiginger (1985,1987).

(b) If production is inflexible expost the firm would do well to hold inventories, and cater to the variable demand at as low a cost as possible. This alternative is the source of the transactions demand for inventory. The significance of such an inventory holding was emphasized in the early work of Holt et al (1960).

Suppose the changes in demand cannot be anticipated with any degree of certainty. As Pindyck (1994) noted, it would then be necessary for the management to set up production targets keeping two considerations in perspective:

(a) the costs of making expost adjustments in production, and
(b) the costs of goodwill associated with being out of stock when the demand arises.

In oligopolistic markets, where market shares are as important as profits from the long run viewpoint[1], the second aspect may be dominant. Hence, firms tend to hold precautionary inventories[2]. For, the cost advantages of production smoothing with a variable inventory stock may be far too little compared to the gains of maintaining a desired inventory stock with variable production schedules[3,4].

---

1. The stability and/or growth of market share can contribute to manager's welfare in the following ways.
(a) It enables the firm to convert market prospects to profits.
(b) It allows the management to recommend itself to the more lucrative jobs it creates, and/or
(c) It can be a deterrent to takeover raids and enhances the job security of the managers.
In sum, a large market share provides the management income, power, and security. This argument is similar to the analysis of Marris (1964) regarding the managerial preference for the growth of capital assets of the firm.

2. Kahn (1987) was the first to develop a model of precautionary demand for inventories when the firm is experiencing demand uncertainty. He demonstrated that the optimal inventory stock varies directly in proportion to
(a) sales, and
(b) the conditional variance of sales.
Also see Kahn (1992), Miron and Zeldes (1988) and Eichenbaum (1979).

3. The desired level of inventory stock need not be a constant proportion of sales. In addition to the unanticipated changes in demand this policy also depends on the uncertainty in cost. For, it would be optimal to increase production when the costs are low and utilize inventory in periods of high costs. See, for instance, Blinder and Maccini (1991 a).

The third aspect which inventory models generally consider is the possibility that inventories can have the effect of increasing the demand for a firm's products and/or making the demand curve more inelastic. For, a large inventory stock of a firm can have the following effects.

(a) It provides the consumer an assurance that the desired supply will be available. Consequently, the demand for the firm's products may increase. See, for instance, Langlois (1989,p.50).

(b) It can deter entry and provide market shelter for the firm. For,

(i) as Phlips (1983,ch.6) argued, the firms which have a large inventory stock may impute higher costs to inventory while maintaining constant output prices thereby under reporting profit opportunities, and/or

(ii) as Ware (1985) pointed out they can sell inventory at a lower price whenever there is a potential threat of entry[5].

The primary aim of inventory in this approach is to increase the profitability of the firm. The speculative inventory has the aim of market share augmentation to achieve this objective[6].

The other important feature of a modern corporation is the decentralized decision making structure which is necessitated by its large size. In such a milieu the inventory decisions are largely in the realm of the production manager who has the task of arranging supply to meet specific sales targets which the

---

4. Blinder (1982) and Blinder and Maccini (1991 a,b) noted that in empirical practice production is more volatile than sales and questioned the validity of the production smoothing model. The economic lot size models which they are trying to resurrect are closely related, but not identical, to the formulation of the decentralized decision processes of the present study.

5. Rao (1991 c) examined these issues in a dynamic framework. The firms gain more from speculative inventory, in comparison to the other two forms, whenever it is possible to influence the demand for its products.

marketing manager sets. It is unrealistic to expect that the production manager would either monitor the emerging changes in the market demand or expects to influence the market share through the changes in the inventory holding[7]. It is more realistic to argue that the precautionary motive is the only dominant consideration in the choice of inventory levels of the firm. In a similar vein the fulfillment of the sales targets is the dominant objective of the decision making process of the production manager. They are constrained to hold inventory to the extent that expost production adjustments, through changes in the laborforce and/or increases in the utilization of the production capacity, are physically infeasible. The cost aspect of such adjustments may also be important in this decision making process but it has only a secondary role. For, while setting the sales targets the marketing manager or the vice president coordinating the activities can be expected to be well aware of these costs. The fundamental departure needed to examine inventory behavior in a decentralized organization consists of acknowledging the precautionary motive directed towards the objective of fulfilling sales targets. The cost considerations alluded to in the conventional literature are unlikely to be important in such a

---

6. Arrow (1958, pp.4-12) contains a detailed description of the three basic motives for holding inventory.

7. In some of the earlier studies the demand for precautionary inventory stock is postulated as a function of expected sales. Then, during any specific interval of time the inventory is expected to adjust to this. See, for instance, Feldstein and Auerbach (1976), Langlois (1989), and Krane (1994). This can be viewed as a formulation of the precautionary demand though there are limitations. The more important difficulty is in assigning a motive for the desired inventory stock to be a function of expected sales. It will be presently shown that this is a constraint on the production manager instead of being a reflection of preferences.

decentralized set up[8].

The primary objective of the present chapter is to test this possibility empirically. The modelling approach proceeds as follows:

(a) It will be postulated that the marketing manager or the vice president of operations monitors the ability of the production division to satisfy the sales target. This is a constraint on the decision making process of the production manager.

(b) Since inventory provides the essential dynamic link for fulfilling sales targets it can be expected that the management considers both sales targets and inventory stock as valuable in their decision making process.

This aspect of managerial discretion is not properly understood in the literature so far.

Therefore an attempt will be made in this study to

(a) reformulate the production inventory decisions on the basis of the economic theory underlying the decentralized decision making process, and

(b) report the empirical results for firms in the chemical industry in the corporate sector.

The rest of the chapter is organized as follows:

(a) section 8.2 details the formulation of the model, and

(b) section 8.3 provides an analysis of the empirical results.

8.2. Modelling Framework

For expository convenience the analysis will be organized along the following lines:

(a) the nature of production inventory decisions,

---

8. In a recent paper, Rao and Rastogi (1995 a) empirically examined managerial motives for holding inventory from the conventional perspective. It was reported that the precautionary motive is more important than the other two.

(b) the constraints on the managerial decisions, and
(c) the structure of managerial preferences.

8.2.1. Short Run Decisions

Consider a firm which is experiencing an uncertain market for its products. The alternative strategies available to the management depend on various factors.

(a) Suppose the orders can be backlogged without incurring any significant goodwill cost. Then, following West (1988), Blinder and Maccini (1991 a), and Krane (1994) it can be argued that the firm should avoid costly inventories and expensive adjustments in production schedules. However, if there are economies of scale in production the firm may hold inventories to reduce the costs of satisfying a given demand. This is the transactions demand for inventory.

(b) In some cases, depending on the extent of competition and the nature of the product, it may be very expensive to backlog orders. Assume that production is flexible expost (i.e., after the uncertainty is resolved) in the sense that the necessary output changes can be brought about at a constant marginal cost. In such a case production will fully adjust to sales targets, without any necessity for backlogging, and there will be no need for any inventory holding. See, for instance, Flacco and Kroetch (1986), Aiginger (1987, p.174), and Krane (1994).

(c) Suppose on the other hand, there is some expost flexibility of production though at an increasing marginal cost. Then some cost saving can be achieved by smoothing production and holding inventories while fulfilling the sales targets. This precautionary demand for inventories was acknowledged in Feldstein and Auerbach (1976), Blinder and Fischer (1981), and Aiginger (1985, p.62).

In sum, the management of a firm can adjust to business risk by backlogging orders, targeting production and/or inventory depending upon the nature of the products and the costs of various

decisions[9]. The two basic short run decisions are
(a) the manpower and compensation policies to ensure the desired production flexibility, and
(b) the inventory to sales ratio.
For, as Glick and Wihlborg (1985), Kahn (1987), Miron and Zeldes (1988), and Eichenbaum (1989) argued, inventory targets are generally proportional to sales. Further, note that the volume of production and the inventory to sales ratio determine the volume of sales during a given interval of time.

8.2.2. The Constraints

From the viewpoint of the vice president in charge of operations the net sales of the firm would generally depend upon
(a) the market conditions,
(b) the production capabilities,
(c) the managerial decisions; especially the personnel and inventory policies,
(d) the constraints implicit in the government policies, and
(e) the constraints imposed by the shareholders.
These aspects are generally interrelated but the potential for generating sales revenue implicit in their variations defines the choices available to the management who value the security afforded by their ability to fulfil sales targets as well as the maintenance of their autonomy. In general, it can be argued that the net sales is determined by
NSAL = f(INSA, WASA, X), where
NSAL = net sales revenue of the firm,
INSA = inventory to sales ratio,

---

9. The preceding argument implies that the demand for inventories is
(a) a transactions demand if the cost of production is the dominant determinant, and
(b) a precautionary demand if the market risks are the driving force.
This provides a useful basis for inference in the empirical work.

WASA = wages and salaries/ cost of goods sold, and
X = a vector of variables which have an effect on the net sales of the firm.

Consider the relationship between NSAL and INSA. Assume that there is an optimal target inventory

$INSA^* = f(NSAL)$

for precautionary purposes. Such an inventory holding can be expected to maximize the sales revenue. The optimal inventory level can be expected to vary with

(a) the size of the firm, due to the economies of scale inherent in large scale production,

(b) the business risks inherent in the product market fluctuations, and

(c) the cost implications of a specific method of finance.

For other values of INSA the changes in NSAL can be determined in the following manner. Suppose the actual INSA is low. Then it can be argued that many opportunities to increase sales exist and the firm can take advantage of them only if the inventory can be suitably increased because production cannot adjust to sales instantaneously. However, a high value of INSA may indicate

(a) a miscalculation about demand leading to unintended inventory accumulation, and/or

(b) an adverse valuation by the consumers of the products of the firm holding excessive inventory either because they expect poor quality or they suspect that high costs will be passed on to them.

NSAL will decrease when $INSA > INSA^*$. In general, the relationship between NSAL and INSA will be of the inverted u-shape.

In a similar fashion, when WASA is low the workers are not motivated to increase production to the possible limits afforded by the expost flexibility. Net sales can be increased by utilizing the production potential if adequate compensation is offered to the workers. However, if WASA increases beyond a limit increases in output, if any, can be obtained only at a high cost. The firm may not be in a position to increase sales per se. Once again an inverted u-shaped relation is expected between WASA and

NSAL.

The maximum NSAL attainable by changing the decisions of the management depends on the X variables as well. Three types of variables are pertinent:

(a) the production capabilities of the firm,

(b) the demand uncertainty, and

(c) the financial risks.

Consider a unit change in WASA and/or INSA which the management contemplates. Normally this would be expected to result in an increase in production. Two possibilities can now be visualized:

(a) there is sufficient production capacity represented by the net fixed assets (NFAS) of the firm and the desired changes can be brought about by taking advantage of the economies of scale, or

(b) NFAS is such that the changes entail steeply increasing marginal costs.

In either case, the change in NSAL for a unit increase in WASA can be written as

$$a_1^* = a_{11} \text{ WASA} + a_{12} \text{ NFAS}$$

Similarly, if INSA increases by one unit, NSAL increases by

$$a_2^* = a_{21} \text{ WASA} + a_{22} \text{ NFAS}$$

so that

$$\text{NSAL} = a_1^* \text{ WASA} + a_2^* \text{ INSA}$$

Note that, given the market conditions, the NSAL maximizing level of WASA and INSA cannot be independent of NFAS. Hence, a constant term is not included in the specification of a_1^* and a_2^*. The maintained hypothesis is that the optimal values of WASA and INSA are functions of NFAS and the other causative factors.

Consider a unit change in the business risk (BSRI). Suppose the management decides to change INSA. Two possibilities should be considered to identify its effect on NSAL :

(a) Suppose the adjustments in INSA are optimal for the given business risk. Then NSAL is a function of INSA alone and BSRI has no further effect.

(b) The adjustment in INSA may accommodate only a part of the change in BSRI. Then it can be argued that the effect on NSAL of a unit change in INSA is given by

$a_1^* = a_{11}$ INSA + a_{12} BSRI

A similar argument holds with respect to the adjustments in WASA which are a result of the changes in BSRI.

Turnovsky (1970) considers financial risk (FIRI) as distinct from BSRI. For, a given choice of WASA and INSA can be financed by different combinations of financial instruments. Rubin (1979), Aiginger (1987, p.69), Blinder and Maccini (1991b, p.82), and Cuthbertson and Gasparro (1993, p.181) argued that the financial strategy of the firm has a major influence on the firm's expected marginal cost of conducting its business during a given interval of time. For, the interest costs of a given method of financing depend upon the financial mix adopted by the firm. The interest costs, which imply a greater repayment committment from the short run cashflow of the firm, must be weighed against the uncertainty in market demand to determine the viability of the decisions.
In general, the following functional form is appropriate :

NSAL = $A_0 + C'A_1C + C'A_2X + A_3Z$, where

C = a (px1) vector of decisions of the management,

X = a (qx1) vector of variables which affect the decisions,

Z = a (sx1) vector of variables which the management considers difficult to accommodate in their decision making though they affect NSAL.

8.2.3. Managerial Preferences

The maintained hypothesis in models of discretionary managerial behavior is that the management associates a positive value with increases in WASA and INSA. For, they increase the security against the loss of goodwill arising from being out of stock. That is, it can be generally postulated that the management would tradeoff sales to attain these objectives. Formally, the preference function can be written as

U = NSAL + λ_1 WASA + λ_2 INSA, where $\lambda_1, \lambda_2 > 0$

However, it can be expected that the management is aware of the possible threats to the viability of the management team brought about by the constraints imposed by the external environment. In particular, the constraints imposed by the shareholders in the form of dividends per share (DIND) can have an effect. It can be expected that the management would reduce the extent of tradeoff depending on DIND. An appropriate specification of the preference function would therefore be

$U = NSAL + \lambda_1^* \, WASA + \lambda_2^* \, INSA$, where

$\lambda_1^* = \lambda_{11} + \lambda_{12} \, DIND$; $\lambda_{11} > 0$, $\lambda_{12} < 0$, and

$\lambda_2^* = \lambda_{21} + \lambda_{22} \, DIND$; $\lambda_{21} > 0$, $\lambda_{22} < 0$

The general form of the preference function would therefore be

$U = NSAL + C'\lambda Y$, where

Y = a (rx1) vector of characteristics representing the constraints and the incentives which the management values.

Note that one of the Y variables in this specification is a constant.

8.3. Empirical Results

The following salient points emerged from the estimates of the INSA equation in Table 8.1.

(a) The size of the fixed assets of the firm and the liquidity problems have only a marginal effect on inventory holding. The transactions demand argument cannot be sustained.

(b) When the business risk is high the firms tend to hold a larger volume of precautionary inventory.

(c) It was postulated that the marketing manager is targetting a sales level and is making efforts to defend it by undertaking wide ranging selling costs. The production manager, in his turn, increases the inventory level to sustain that position. Ten firms exhibited this pattern.

(d) The financial risk implied by the interest payments obligations and the debt repayment requirements place an effective constraint on the propensity to hold excessive inventory.

(e) The pressure to pay adequate dividends is the most important deterrent on excessive inventory holding in most cases.

Though the inventory decisions of Borax and Morrisons are not systematically influenced by these variables they do hold a substantial inventory.

Consider the estimated WASA equation presented in Table 8.2. The following observations are pertinent:

(a) Large firms are either capital intensive and/or they do not generally have any problems in attracting the requisite laborforce. Invariably their wage bill as a proportion of total cost decreases with size.

(b) Higher corporate taxes deter the firms from incurring large fixed costs of wage payments. TAXT has a negative influence on WASA.

(c) The fixed cost nature of wages also makes them sensitive to dividend payments requirements.

(d) When the business risks are high firms are compelled to either hold large precautionary inventory or adjust production continuously to respond to the market fluctuations. In both these cases they find it necessary to increase WASA as BSRI increases.

(e) The higher risks associated with debt repayments and financial risks do put a limit on the extent to which the fixed costs associated with WASA can be increased.

Turning to the NSAL equation it should be noted that

(a) 17 firms in the sample hold excessive inventory. Clearly, they do not have the expost production flexibility alluded to in Aiginger (1987).

(b) Six firms spend excessive amounts on personnel and depend on adjusting production to changing business conditions.

(c) The rest of the firms do not exhibit any clear preference for INSA or WASA.

Refer to Table 8.3. The estimated NSAL equation for the 17 firms which exhibited a preference for excessive inventory revealed the following trends.

(a) Most of the firms find it difficult to adjust the inventory level fully to the selling expenses incurred by the marketing manager.

(b) The size of the firm, as reflected in the capital assets of the firm, is an important determinant of the sales revenue of the firm though it has no direct bearing on the inventory choice of the firm.

(c) The firms are sensitive to the cost implications, represented by DEBT and FIRI, in their choice of the inventory to sales ratio.

(d) Large business risks induce the management of some firms to adjust INSA but generally the adjustment is not optimal due to cost considerations. As a result BSRI has an influence on NSAL.

Consider the managerial preferences of this group of firms as reported in Table 8.4. The following aspects are noteworthy:

(a) They hold inventories in excess of those necessary to defend the sales maximization requirement.

(b) Many firms find DIND an effective constraint in making them reduce the tradeoff between sales revenue and precautionary inventory holdings.

Table 8.5 provides the estimated NSAL equations for the firms which have a preference for WASA. Clearly these firms have some ex post flexibility in production which they wish to utilize. This will reduce their inventory holding costs. These firms exhibit the following patterns:

(a) They adjust WASA to the volume of net fixed assets and perhaps maintain a sufficiently large workforce to achieve production flexibility.

(b) The other significant aspect is that they adjust WASA to business risk in their efforts to adjust production to the market.

(c) These firms are not particularly influenced by the cost effects though LIQD and TAXT had some influence in the case of Morrisons and Union Carbide.

The managerial preferences of such firms, as exhibited in Table 8.6, suggest that in a majority of cases their propensity to spend more on wages and salaries to maintain expost production flexibility is tempered by the dividend constraints.

Table 8.7 contains the expansion path estimates for the rest of the firms. Their sales are mostly proportional to the size of the fixed assets. There is no evidence of excessive inventory or excessive manpower in the case of such firms.

In general it can be concluded that

(a) most firms prefer to adjust to the sales targets by holding precautionary inventory.

(b) Most firms do not have adequate ex post production flexibility. Such firms hold excessive inventory. They are sensitive to cost effects.

(c) Some firms are not bound by the cost constraints. Such firms tend to spend excessively on personnel and maintain expost production flexibility.

(d) Most of the firms are sensitive to the dividend constraint in their decision making process.

Table 8.1. The INSA Equation

S.No	Firm	Cons	BSRI	FIRI	NFAS	GNEX	LIQD
1.	ALB	0.25	-	-	-	-	-
		(0.021)					
2.	ALEM	0.35	-	-2.27	-	-	-
		(0.045)		(1.07)			
3.	ARL	-0.084	0.25	-	0.058	-	0.43
		(0.19)	(0.082)		(0.021)		(0.16)
4.	BASF	0.12	-	-	-	0.38	-
		(0.040)				(0.22)	
5.	BAYER	0.24	0.16	-	-	0.30	-
		(0.036)	(0.076)			(0.14)	
6.	BOOTS	0.26	-0.16	-	-	-	-
		(0.018)	(0.11)				
7.	COCHIN	0.10	0.094	-	-	-	-
		(0.011)	(0.018)				
8.	COLOR	0.34	-	-1.51	-	-	-
		(0.031)		(0.62)			
9.	CORO	0.19	-	-	-	0.23	-
		(0.027)				(0.19)	
10.	DCW	0.32	-0.33	-	-	-	-
		(0.21)	(0.098)				
11.	DHM	0.24	-	-0.85	-	-	-
		(0.018)		(0.347)			
12.	DYES	0.42	-	-	-	-	-
		(0.030)					
13.	GLAXO	0.38	-	-2.29	-	-0.33	-
		(0.043)		(0.94)		(0.16)	
14.	GUJ	0.18	-	-	-	-	0.053
		(0.061)					(0.027)
15.	HERDIL	0.23	-	-	-	3.12	-
		(0.079)				(1.54)	
16.	IDL	0.30	-	-1.34	-	-	-
		(0.026)		(0.45)			

Table 8.1 (contd)

17.	KANOR	0.28	-	-	-	-	-
		(0.021)					
18.	NOCIL	0.089	0.32	-	-	1.08	-
		(0.026)	(0.086)			(0.36)	
19.	POLY	0.13	-	5.03	0.049	6.65	-
		(0.14)		(1.86)	(0.0025)	(2.44)	
20.	RALLIS	0.16	0.14	-	-	-	-
		(0.012)	(0.063)				
21.	SANDOZ	0.21	-	-	-	0.62	-
		(0.067)				(0.30)	
22.	SYNTH	0.26	-	-	-	1.15	-
		(0.038)				(0.29)	
23.	TATA	0.33	-	-	*	-	-
		(0.013)				-	-
24.	UNICHEM	0.24	-	-	-	-	-
		(0.24)					
25.	UNION	0.059	0.19	-	-	1.57	-
		(0.040)	(0.093)			(0.48)	

Notes :

Figures in the brackets are the standard errors.

There was no significant explanation for the inventory holding of BORAX and JLM (Morrisons).

* This figure is 0.000096 and correspondingly the standard error is 0.000093.

Table 8.1. (contd)

DEBT	DIND	R^2
-	-0.0072	0.94
	(0.0031)	
	-	0.97
-0.82	-0.012	0.95
(0.027)	(0.0033)	
-	-	0.96
-	-0.0045	0.99
	(0.00084)	
-	-	0.98
-	-	0.91
-	-	0.97
-	-	0.94
-	-0.0020	0.95
	(0.0011)	
-	-	0.94
-0.041	-0.0072	0.98
(0.016)	(0.0019)	
-	-	0.96
-	-	0.88
-0.19	-0.083	0.88
(0.074)	(0.024)	
-	-0.038	0.95
	(0.015)	

Table 8.1 (contd)

-0.040	-	0.96
(0.015)		
-	-	0.96
-	-0.028	0.68
	(0.0092)	
-	-	0.97
-0.13	-	0.96
(0.068)		
-	-	0.88
-	-	0.95
-	-	0.97
-0.17	-	0.96
(0.045)		

Table 8.2. The WASA Equation

S.No	Firm	Cons	BSRI	FIRI	NFAS	GNEX
1.	ALB	0.078	0.58	-	-	-
		(0.0084)	(0.026)			
2.	ALEM	0.70	-	-2.45	-0.0044	-0.23
		(0.0077)		(0.69)	(0.0011)	(0.11)
3.	ARL	0.12	0.047	-	-	-
		(0.0077)	(0.015)			
4.	BASF	0.28	-	-	-	-
		(0.020)				
5.	BAYER	0.20	-	-	-0.00057	-
		(0.0091)			(0.00027)	
6.	BOOTS	0.28	-	-0.50	-0.0034	-
		(0.0069)		(0.31)	(0.00068)	
7.	BORAX	0.094	0.081	-	-0.0058	-
		(0.0028)	(0.011)		(0.0010)	
8.	COCHIN	0.012	-	-	-	-
		(0.0015)				
9.	COLOR	0.14	-	-	-	-
		(0.0070)				
10.	CORO	0.085	-	-	-0.00017	-
		(0.0048)			(0.000049)	
11.	DCW	0.20	-	-	-	-
		(0.10)				
12.	DHM	0.14	-0.066	-	-	-
		(0.014)	(0.022)			
13.	DYES	0.12	-	-	-	-
		(0.0052)				
14.	GLAXO	0.32	-	-	-	-
		(0.022)				
15.	GUJ	0.11	-0.048	-	-	-
		(0.010)	(0.022)			
16.	HERDIL	0.11	-	-	-	-
		(0.0053)				

Table 8.2 (contd)

17.	IDL	0.30	-	-	-0.0019	-
		(0.019)			(0.00073)	
18.	JLM	0.25	-	-	-0.052	-
		(0.023)			(0.025)	
19.	KANOR	0.27	-	-1.67	-0.00048	-
		(0.033)		(0.060)	(0.00023)	
20.	NOCIL	0.076	0.10	-	-	-
		(0.0093)	(0.024)			
21.	POLY	0.090	-	-	-	-
		(0.0060)				
22.	RALLIS	0.076	0.042	-	-	-
		(0.0048)	(0.024)			
23.	SANDOZ	0.40	0.17	-	-	-
		(0.034)	(0.083)			
24.	SYNTH	0.21	0.12	-0.92	-0.00078	-
		(0.025)	(0.033)	(0.55)	(0.00037)	
25.	TATA	0.20	-	-	-	-
		(0.015)				
26.	UNICHM	0.22	-	-	-0.0041	-
		(0.0064)			(0.0010)	
27.	UNION	0.23	-	-	-0.0018	-
		(0.042)			(0.00038)	

Table 8.2 (contd)

LIQD	TAXT	DEBT	DIND	R^2
-	-	-	-	0.96
-0.27 (0.091)	-0.076 (0.027)	-	-	0.99
-	-	-	-0.0015 (0.00034)	0.96
-	-0.14 (0.038)	-0.035 (0.015)	-0.0041 (0.0013)	0.96
-	-0.11 (0.18)	-	-	0.99
-	-	-0.050 (0.16)	-	0.99
-	-	-	-	0.99
-	-0.014 (0.0035)	-0.00035 (0.00017)	-	0.81
-	-0.081 (0.016)	-	-	0.99
-	-0.035 (0.010)	-	-	0.97
-	-	-	-0.0034 (0.00059)	0.96
-	-	-	-0.0025 (0.0014)	0.99
-	-0.034 (0.015)	-	-	0.97
-	-	-0.17 (0.032)	-0.029 (0.015)	0.98
-	-	-	-0.0014 (0.00038)	0.96
-	-0.029 (0.014)	-	-	0.97

Table 8.2 (contd)

-	-0.11 (0.032)	-	-	0.99
-	-	-	-	0.96
-	-	-	-	0.96
-	-	-	-0.00066 (0.00033)	0.96
-	-0.024 (0.016)	-	-	0.95
-	-	-	-	0.98
-	-	-	-0.18 (0.024)	0.98
-	-	-	-0.0052 (0.0012)	0.96
-	-	-	-0.033 (0.0068)	0.98
-	-	-	-	0.99
-	-	-	-	0.99

Table 8.3. NSAL(INSA) Equation

S.No	Firm	Cons	INSA2	ISBRI	IFIRI	IDEBT
1.	ALB	30.50	-374.70	-	-	-
		(8.03)	(144.50)			
2.	ALEM	551.00	-4623.00	-	-20930.00	-
		(97.70)	(880.50)		(3987.00)	
3.	BASF	0.043	-10.13	-	-	-
		(0.042)	(3.68)			
4.	BAYER	0.031	-0.81	0.25	-	-
		(0.013)	(0.37)	(0.12)		
5.	BOOTS	0.42	-6.57	-2.06	-	-
		(0.13)	(0.05)	(0.64)		
6.	COLOR	0.43	-4.54	-	-13.60	-
		(0.11)	(0.48)		(2.96)	
7.	DCW	0.086	-1.04	-0.70	-	-
		(0.036)	(0.31)	(0.20)		
8.	DHM	0.29	-4.93	-	-8.37	-
		(0.17)	(2.81)		(4.77)	
9.	DYES	0.12	-2.12	-	-	-0.17
		(0.056)	(0.45)			(0.037)
10.	HERDIL	0.0056	-0.32	-	-	-0.12
		(0.0075)	(0.15)			(0.056)
11.	IDL	114.00	-879.30	-	-2352.00	-
		(16.60)	(249.10)		(666.10)	
12.	KANOR	0.69	-9.35	-	-	-0.75
		(0.091)	(1.09)			(0.088)
13.	NOCIL	-0.088	-2.69	1.70	-	-
		(0.027)	(0.75)	(0.48)		
14.	POLY	26.20	-633.90	-	-13590.00	-
		(21.40)	(89.92)		(1927.00)	
15.	SANDOZ	0.16	-1.81	-	-	-0.48
		(0.053)	(0.76)			(0.20)
16.	SYNTH	0.25	-0.51	-	-	-
		(0.047)	(0.19)			

Table 8.3 (contd)

17.	UNICHM	0.096	-1.70	-	-	-0.59
		(0.026)	(0.46)			(0.16)

Note: The interaction terms in the table are

INSA2 = $INSA^2$

IBSRI = INSA x BSRI

IFIRI = INSA x FIRI

IDEBT = INSA x DEBT

INFAS = INSA x NFAS

IGNEX = INSA x GNEX

WASA2 = $WASA^2$

Table 8.3 (contd)

INFAS	IGNEX	BSRI	FIRI	DEBT	NFAS
-	-	-	-	-	-
-	-	-	-	-	-
-	7.75	-	-	-0.051	-
	(2.81)			(0.017)	
-	0.49	-	-	-	-
	(0.22)				
-	-	-	-	-	0.0075
					(0.00030)
-	-	-	-	-	-
-	-	-	-0.91	-	0.0013
			(0.29)		(0.00010)
-	-	-	-	-0.029	-
				(0.0098)	
-	-	-	-	-	-
-	1.96	-	-	-	0.0026
	(0.93)				(0.00026)
-	-	-	-	-	-
-	-	-	-1.20	-	-
			(0.36)		
-	5.81	-	-1.61	-0.39	0.0063
	(1.63)		(0.53)	(0.017)	(0.0017)
13.10	4994.00	118.40	-	-	-
(1.86)	(708.30)	(69.82)			
-	2.25	-	-	-	0.0077
	(0.94)				(0.00093)
-	1.17	-	-	-	-
	(0.45)				

Table 8.3 (contd)

-	-	0.025	-	-	0.0043
		(0.012)			(0.00045)

Table 8.3. (contd)

LIQD	TAXT	WASA	WASA2	DIND	R^2
-	-10.37 (6.39)	-	-	-	0.21
-	-	-	-	-	0.60
0.16 (0.033)	-	-	-	-	0.51
-	-	-	-	-	0.93
-	-	-	-	-	0.97
-	-	-	-	0.0081 (0.00073)	0.90
0.062 (0.019)	-0.040 (0.013)	-	-	-	0.97
-	-0.013 (0.0072)	-	-	0.0017 (0.00093)	0.99
-	-	-	12.99 (2.30)	-	0.70
-	-	-	-	-	0.87
-	-75.02 (16.93)	-	-	-	0.55
0.096 (0.032)	-	-	-	-	0.76
-	-	-	-	-	0.94
-	-	-	-	-	0.70
-	-	-0.52 (0.15)	-	-	0.90
-	-	-1.40 (0.33)	-	-	0.43

Table 8.3 (contd)

-	-	-	-	-	0.94

Table 8.4. λ(INSA) Estimates

S.No	Firm	INSA	IDIND
1.	ALB	185.45	-5.37
		(71.51)	(2.07)
2.	ALEM	3201.00	-
		(609.80)	
3.	BASF	2.43	-
		(0.88)	
4.	BAYER	0.40	-0.0073
		(0.18)	(0.0033)
5.	BOOTS	3.36	-
		(1.05)	
6.	COLOR	3.08	-
		(0.67)	
7.	DCW	0.67	-0.0042
		(0.20)	(0.0012)
8.	DHM	2.41	-
		(1.37)	
9.	DYES	1.76	-0.030
		(0.37)	(0.0064)
10.	HERD	0.14	-0.052
		(0.068)	(0.025)
11.	IDL	527.50	-66.06
		(149.40)	(18.71)
12.	KANOR	5.22	-
		(0.61)	
13.	NOCIL	0.48	-
		(0.13)	
14.	POLY	747.00	-50.73
		(106.00)	(7.20)
15.	SANDOZ	0.77	-
		(0.32)	
16.	SYNTH	0.26	-
		(0.10)	

Table 8.4 (contd)

17.	UNICHM	0.81 (0.22)	-

Note : The interaction term in the table is
DIND = INSA x DIND

Table 8.5. NSAL(WASA) Equation

S.No	Firm	Cons	WASA	WBSRI	WNFAS	WDEBT
1.	ARL	5.97	-403.50	38.15	-	-
		(2.05)	(152.90)	(14.45)		
2.	GLAXO	702.00	-7871.00	-	-	-2685.00
		(112.00)	(1587.00)			(541.20)
3.	GUJ	451.00	-45490.00	-4650.00	-	-
		(83.00)	(9722.00)	(993.00)		
4.	JLM	92.20	-1488.00	-	-155.10	-
		(6.50)	(97.46)		(10.22)	
5.	TATA	216.00	-9769.00	-	-	-
		(28.00)	(1425.00)			
6.	UNION	1000.00	-17810.00	-	-64.24	-
		(225.00)	(4428.00)		(15.47)	

Note: The interaction terms in the table are

WBSRI = WASA x BSRI

WNFAS = WASA x NFAS

WDEBT = WASA x DEBT

Table 8.5 (contd)

FIRI	NFAS	DEBT	LIQD	TAXT	DIND	R^2
-	2.39	-	-	-	-	0.97
	(0.22)					
-	-	-	-	-	-	0.52
-	0.9120	-	-	-	-	0.88
	(0.1132)					
-53.49	-	-	5.61	-17.76	8.54	0.98
(27.55)			(2.58)	(1.91)	(0.96)	
-	0.53	-	-	-	-	0.95
	(0.055)					
-	-	-133.80	72.20	-104.00	-	0.73
		(33.17)	(14.29)	(39.46)		

Table 8.6. λ(WASA) Estimates

S.No	Firm	WASA	WDIND
1.	ARL	96.96	-1.17
		36.73)	(0.44)
2.	GLAXO	5036.00	-347.70
		(1015.00)	(92.27)
3.	GUJ	10390.00	-121.40
		(2220.00)	(25.94)
4.	JLM	744.60	-
		(49.03)	
5.	TATA	3835.00	-638.90
		(559.40)	(93.20)
6.	UNION	8223.00	-
		(2044.00)	

Note: The interaction term in the table is
WDIND = WASA x DIND

Table 8.7. NSAL (Expansion Path) Estimates

S.No	Firm	Cons	BSRI	NFAS	R^2
1.	BORAX	-0.0029	-	0.0060	0.93
		(0.0012)		(0.00056)	
2.	COCHIN	0.19	-0.25	0.0042	0.92
		(0.063)	(0.083)	(0.00039)	
3.	CORO	0.017	-	0.0016	0.92
		(0.015)		(0.00018)	
4.	RALLIS	0.076	-	0.0078	0.98
		(0.014)		(0.00058)	

CHAPTER 9

IN RETROSPECT

9.1. The Theoretical Progress

The theory of the firm, as of today, acknowledges three sources of managerial discretion.

(a) Almost every firm in the oligopolistic market environment derives a profit from its operations at least in the short run. They also generate non-price strategies to maintain or augment these profits dynamically. The existence of positive profits is usually one of the necessary conditions for the discretionary use of resources by the management.

(b) Firms can be expected to pursue certain dynamic objectives. For instance, in oligopolistic markets, maintaining the market share to stay ahead of competition would have necessitated foregoing some of the profits. Similarly, even when the firm generates maximum possible profits it may be compelled to pay the workers and the lenders a part of the profits to ensure long run survival. In other words, managerial discretion manifests itself at the level of distribution of net gains.

(c) In practice, most of the large firms have decentralized organizational structures. This is a consequence of the information overload. However, decentralization results in

(i) asymmetric information at the various decision levels,

(ii) adverse selection, and

(iii) moral hazard.

None of the managers of the decentralized divisions has the information to pursue centralized objectives like the profit or value maximization. In addition, there is a possibility that the managers of the firm can exercise authority and pursue personal goals in preference to corporate objectives. Such managerial discretion can be expected to generate utility to the management in excess of the cost imposed on the shareholders.

In the more recent literature on organizational economics the emphasis has been on the third approach. This is expected to provide the most practical insights into the internal functioning of the firm, the relationships between the different organizational echelons, and the conditioning effects of organizational controls and the market environment external to the firm. However, the theoretical approaches have been basically confined to the aggregate level and pursue one of two possible themes.

One of these is the frontier production or profit function approach. The conceptualization here emphasizes the possibility that the managerial decisions in the actual operation of the firm result in performance below the potential maximum. The X-inefficiency literature developed by Leibenstein (1980), and Hoenack's (1983) description of resource diversions are typical examples. Following the lead from Farrell (1957) many authors, including Sengupta (1988,1995) are making attempts to empirically evaluate this aspect of the problem. The second approach assumes that the decisions are along the efficient frontier but the management exhibits a tradeoff between profit and other objectives of personal interest. The uncertainty regarding the usefulness of one of these approaches over the other can be best summarized through the following quotation from Barney and Ouchi (1986, p.24) " Minor modifications that lead to revolutionary conclusions are characteristic of much of the work on organizational economics. Authors make what appear to be minor alterations in traditional theory, only to generate significantly different and somewhat surprising conclusions."

The present study took the second perspective. Even in this context the emphasis can be at different levels. Some attempts are under progress to examine the influence of organizational structures and control mechanisms on the efficiency of managerial decisions and corporate performance. Much of this literature emphasizes the differences across firms. Cable (1988), and Hill (1984) offer comprehensive surveys of this literature. Rao and Saha (1995 a,b) represent the only known studies along these lines in the Indian context.

However, this study was somewhat more amibitious. It takes the decision making process of each of the firms in isolation and delves into the objectives of the different decentralized levels of the management. The broad maintained hypotheses and the basic insights obtained from the empirical analysis can be summarized thus:

(a) There is a general agreement that the management's choice of the capital assets of the firm and portfolio diversification (in particular, the choice of the debt equity ratio) provides them a certain amount of corporate control. The management values control keeping the constraining effect of the market value of the firm in perspective. The empirical evidence of the present study indicates that the managers express a preference either for the growth of capital assets or the control implied by the choice of the debt equity ratio. They are, however, averse to taking the risks of financing excessive growth by a high debt equity ratio. That is, the bonding effects are significant even if there is an element of discretion in the long term choices of the management.

(b) The marketing managers of decentralized firms have a tendency to target a lower than profit maximizing level of the market share and indulge in excessive selling costs. In contrast to the existing studies, which emphasize the market structure as the major source of excessive advertising, the behavior of the management in decentralized organizations is independent of the product market.

(c) In the context of decentralized organizations the more realistic objective for the production manager is to choose the personnel and inventory policies to fulfill the sales targets set by the marketing manager. Inventories will then be mostly precautionary and tend to be excessive if the management is risk averse.

While the present study represents a significant progress towards understanding the behavior of the managers at different levels in a decentralized organization there are several theoretical issues that have yet to be resolved. The following aspects are representative.

(a) How autonomous is each of the divisions? In particular, what is the extent of freedom in the choice of decisions, their

execution, and obtaining finances to implement their decisions?
(b) Can the proximate objectives of each of the decisions be specified in such a way that there is no overlap between them?
(c) How can a theoretical structure be specified to understand the coordination function of the higher level manager?

It should be reiterated that a great deal of theoretical research along these dimensions is warranted.

9.2. Issues of Model Specification

In general, there are wide ranging interrelationships between the C, X, and Y variables of the model specification. In particular, it is evident that some of the Y variables are decisions of a higher level of management. Similarly, the market variables X may themselves be influenced by the choice of C. The classification of any given variable is an analytical judgement based on the specific purpose for which the model is constructed.

The more difficult problem is this. Just as a decision model was formulated for C a similar model for the choices of Y can be formulated. Simultaneous estimation of such models would be a formidable task.

The models of the present study assumed that there are instantaneous adjustments in C to the variations in the X and Y variables. Perhaps it would be more realistic to expect lagged values of X and/or Y to have the basic influence on C. To introduce time lags into the model a preliminary decision must be made about the classification into the X and Y category. Irrespective of this decision it is necessary to address the estimation problems involved.

The present study assumed that the firm utilizes the same control structure throughout the time period of the study. However, it should be possible to investigate the changes made over time if any. The switching regression methods will be useful in such a context.

9.3. Estimation Problems

The empirical specification of the valuation frontier and the preference function can be at best approximate. It would be reasonable to include a random error term in the equation depicting the strategic choices. However, this may not strictly represent a decision error in the sense of Chow (1983). Even in such a case, treating the estimates of B_1, and B_2 as stochastic and restructuring the test procedure using asymptotic normality as in Rao (1965) would perhaps be justified.

The strategic decisions, as represented by the reduced form
$C = B_1X + B_2Y$,
are simultaneous decisions of the management. Hence, they will have the form of Zellner's seemingly unrelated regressions. It may be useful to modify the estimation procedure accordingly.

9.4. Conclusion

The present study is a basic contribution to the theoretical modelling, methodological and estimation procedures, and empirical insights into the nature and operation of managerial discretion in decentralized organizations. The most important progress in the future must be along the theoretical dimension. In particular, the identification of the proximate objectives of the different levels of management, the specific constraints on their decisions, and the incentives offered to the different levels of management need attention. The estimation procedures outlined in the study are also fundamental. However, a further investigation of the identification problem in optimizing models of this nature is warranted.

REFERENCES

Agarwal,A., and G.N.Mandlekar (1987), Managerial Incentives and Corporate Investment and Financing Decisions, Journal of Finance, 42, 823-838.

Aiginger,K. (1985), The Impact of Risk Attitude, Uncertainty and Disequilibria on Optimal Production and Inventory, Theory and Decision, 19, 51-75.

Aiginger,K. (1987), Production and Decision Theory Under Uncertainty (Oxford: Basil Blackwell).

Arrow,K.J. (1958), Historical Background, in K.J.Arrow, S.Karlin, and H.Scarf (eds.) Studies in the Mathemetical Theory of Inventory and Production (Stanford: Stanford University Press).

Balasubramanian,N. (1993), Corporate Financial Policies and Shareholder Returns: The Indian Experience (Bombay: Himalaya).

Barney,J.B. (1986), Review of Economic Behavior within Organizations, Administrative Science Quarterly, 31, 140-142.

Barney,J.B., and W.G.Ouchi (1986), Organizational Economics (SanFransisco: Jossey Bass).

Bardsley,P. (1975), Optimal Leverage for the Utility Maximizing Firm, Journal of Economic Behavior and Organization, 26, 237-251.

Bartlett,C.A., and S.Ghoshal (1987), Managing Across Borders: New Organizational Responses, Sloan Management Review, 29, 43-53.

Basu,K. (1993), Lectures in Industrial Organization Theory (Oxford: Basil Blackwell).

Bates,J., and J.R.Parkinson (1982), Business Economics (Oxford: Basil Blackwell).

Baumol,W.J. (1959), Business Behavior, Value and Growth (NewYork: Macmillan).

Baumol,W.J., J.Panzar, and R.D.Willig (1982), Contestable Markets and the Theory of Industrial Structure (NewYork: Harcourt).

Benston,G. (1985), The Self-Serving Management Hypothesis: Some Evidence, Journal of Accounting and Economics, 7, 67-84.

Berle,A.A., and G.C.Means (1932), The Modern Corporation and Private Property (NewYork: Harcourt).

Blinder,A.S. (1982), Inventories and Sticky Prices: More on the Microfoundations of Macroeconomics, American Economic Review, 72, 334-348.

Blinder,A.S., and S.Fischer (1981), Inventories, Rational Expectations, and the Business Cycle, Journal of Monetary Economics, 8, 277-304.

Blinder,A.S., and L.Maccini (1991 a), The Resurgence of Inventory Research: What Have We Learned?, Journal of Economic Surveys, 5, 291-328.

Blinder,A.S., and L.Maccini (1991 b), Taking Stock: A Critical Assessment of Recent Research on Inventories, Journal of Economic Perspectives, 5, 73-96.

Bolton,P., and J.Farrell (1990), Decentralization, Duplication, and Delay, Journal of Political Economy, 98, 803-820.

Burton,R.M., and B.Obel (1984), Designing Efficient Organizations: Modelling and Experimentation (Amsterdam: North Holland).

Cable,J.R. (1988), Organization Form and Economic Performance, in S.Thompson and M.Wright (eds.) Internal Organization, Efficiency, and Profit (Oxford: Phillip Allen).

Carlton,D.W. (1978), Vertical Integration in Competitive Markets Under Uncertainty, American Economic Review, 68, 571-587.

Castanias,R.P., and C.E.Helfat (1992), Managerial and Windfall Rents in the Market for Corporate Control, Journal of Economic Behavior and Organization, 18, 153-185.

Chamberlin, E.H. (1962), The Theory of Monopolistic Competition (Cambridge: Harvard University Press).

Chandler,A.D. (1962), Strategy and Structure: Chapters in the History of the Industrial Enterprise (Cambridge: M.I.T.Press).

Chandler,A.D. (1990), Scale and Scope (Cambridge: Balknap Press of the Harvard University).

Chang,C. (1992), Capital Structure as an Optimal Contract Between Employees and Investors, Journal of Finance, 47, 1141-1158.

Chang,S.J., and U.Choi (1988), Strategy, Structure and Performance of Korean Business Groups, Journal of Industrial Economics, 37, 141-158.

Chow,G.C. (1983), Econometrics (NewYork: Wiley).

Clemens,E.W. (1951), Price Discrimination and the Multiproduct Firm, Review of Economic Studies, 19, 1-11.

Coase,R. (1937), The Nature of the Firm, Economica, 4, 386-405.

Colling,T., and A.Ferner (1992), The Limits of Autonomy:

Devolution, Line Managers and Industrial Relations in Privatized Companies, Journal of Management Studies, 29, 209-227.

Comanor,W.S., and T.A.Wilson (1979), The Effect of Advertising on Competition: A Survey, Journal of Economic Literature, 17, 453-476.

Conyon,M.J., and D.Leech (1994), Top Pay, Company Performance and Corporate Governance, Oxford Bulletin of Economics and Statistics, 56, 229-247.

Copeland,T.E., and J.F.Weston (1988), Financial Theory and Corporate Policy (Menlo Park: Addison-Wesley).

Coughlan,A.T., and R.H.Schmidt (1985), Executive Compensation, Management Turnover, and Firm Performance: An Empirical Investigation, Journal of Accounting and Economics, 7, 43-66.

Coughlan,A.T., and S.K.Sen (1989), Sales Compensation: Theory and Managerial Implications, Marketing Science, 8, 324-342.

Cubbin,J., and D.Leech (1983), The Effect of Shareholding Dispersion on the Degree of Control in British Companies: Theory and Measurement, Economic Journal, 93, 351-369.

Cubbin,J., and D.Leech (1986), Growth Versus Profit Maximization: A Simultaneous Equations Approach to Testing the Marris Model, Managerial and Decision Economics, 7, 123-131.

Cuthbertson,K., and D.Gasparro (1993), The Determinants of Manufacturing Inventories in the U.K., Economic Journal, 103, 1479-1492.

Cyert,R.M., and J.G.March (1963), A Behavioral Theory of the Firm (Engelwood Cliffs: Prentice Hall).

DeAlessi,L. (1983), Property Rights, Transaction Costs, and X-Efficiency: An Essay in Economic Theory, American Economic Review, 73, 64-81.

DeAlessi,L., and R.P.Fishe (1987), Why do Corporations Distribute Assets? An Analysis of Dividends and Capital Structure, Journal of Institutional and Theoretical Economics, 143, 34-51.

DeAlessi,L., and R.J.Staff (1987), Liability, Control, and Organization of Economic Activity, International Review of Law and Economics, 7, 5-20.

Dixit,A., and V.Norman (1978), Advertising and Welfare, Bell

Journal of Economics, 9, 1-17.

Donaldson,H. (1987), Strategy and Structural Adjustment to Regain Fit and Performance: In Defence of Contingency Theory, Journal of Management Studies, 24, 1-24.

Dow,G.K. (1988), Information, Production Decisions, and Intra-Firm Bargaining, International Economic Review, 29, 57-79.

Drucker,P.F. (1986), The Practice of Management (NewYork: Harper and Row).

Easterbrook,F.H. (1984), Two Agency-Cost Explanations of Dividends, American Economic Review, 74, 650-660.

Eckard,E.W. (1987), Advertising, Competition, and Market Share Stability, Journal of Business, 60, 539-552.

Edwards,F.R. (1977), Managerial Objectives in Regulated Industries: Expense Preference Behavior in Banking, Journal of Political Economy, 85, 147-162.

Eichenbaum,M.S. (1989), Some Empirical Evidence on the Production Level and Production Cost Smoothing Model of Inventory Investment, American Economic Review, 79, 853-864.

Fama,E.F. (1990), Contract Costs and Financing Decisions, Journal of Business, 63, S 71- S 92.

Fama,E.F., and M.C.Jensen (1983), Seperation of Ownership and Control, Journal of Law and Economics, 26, 301-325.

Farrell,M.J. (1957), The Measurement of Productive Efficiency, Journal of the Royal Statistical Society, Series A, 120, 253-290.

Fazzari,S.M., and B.C.Peterson (1993), Working Capital and Fixed Investment: New Evidence on Financing Constraints, Rand Journal of Economics, 24, 328-342.

Feldstein,M.S., and A.J.Auerbach (1976), Inventory Behavior in Durable Goods Manufacturing: The Target-Adjustment Model, Brookings Papers on Economic Activity, 2, 351-396.

Filippi,E., and G.Zanetti (1971), Exogenous and Endogenous Factors in the Growth of Firms, in R.Marris and A.Wood (eds.) The Corporate Economy (Cambridge: Harvard University Press).

Fisher,F.O., R.Heinekel, and J.Zechner (1989), Dynamic Capital Structure Choice: Theory and Tests, Journal of Finance, 44, 19-40.

FitzRoy,F.R., and K.Kraft (1987), Efficiency and Internal

Organization: Workers Councils in West German Firms, Economica, 54, 493-504.

Flacco,P.R., and B.G.Kroetch (1986), Adjustment to Production Uncertainty and the Theory of the Firm, Economic Inquiry, 24, 485-495.

Flath,D., and C.R.Knober (1985), Managerial Shareholding, Journal of Industrial Economics, 34, 93-100.

Francis,A. (1980), Company Objectives, Managerial Motivations and the Behavior of Large Firms: An Empirical Test of the Theory of Managerial Capitalism, Cambridge Journal of Economics, 4, 349-361.

Friend,I., and L.Lang (1988), An Empirical Test of the Impact of Managerial Self-interest on Corporate Capital Structure, Journal of Finance, 43, 271-281.

Garvey,G., and N.Gaston (1991), Delegation, the Role of Managerial Discretion as a Bonding Device, and the Enforcement of Implicit Contracts, Advances in Econometrics, 9, 87-120.

Gaynor,M. (1989), Competition Within the Firm: Theory Plus Some Evidence from Medical Group Practice, Rand Journal of Economics, 20, 59-76.

Glazer,J., and R.Israel (1990), Managerial Incenties and Financial Signalling in Product Market Competition, International Journal of Industrial Organization, 8, 271-280.

Glete,J. (1989), Long-Term Firm Growth and Ownership Organization, Journal of Economic Behavior and Organization, 12, 329-351.

Glick,R., and C.Wihlborg (1985), Price and Output Adjustment, Inventory Flexibility, and the Cost and Demand Distrubances, Canadian Journal of Economics, 18, 566-573.

Grabowski,H.G., and D.C.Mueller (1972), Managerial and Shareholder Welfare Models of Firm Expenditures, Review of Economics and Statistics, 54, 9-24.

Gravelle,H.S. (1982), Incentives, Efficiency and Control in Public Firms, Zeitschrift fur Nationalokonomie, 42, 79-104.

Green,R.C., and E.Talmor (1986), Asset Substitution and the Agency Costs of Debt Financing, Journal of Banking and Finance, 10, 391-399.

Grossman,S.J., and O.D.Hart (1982), Corporate Financial Structure and Managerial Incentives, in J.J.McCall (ed.) The Economics of

Information and Uncertainty (Chicago: Chicago University Press).

Hamilton,T.R., and S.G.Shergill (1992), The Relationship Between Strategy-Structure Fit and Financial Performance in NewZealand, Journal of Management Studies, 29, 95-113.

Harris,M., and A.Raviv (1988), Corporate Control Contests and Capital Structure, Journal of Financial Economics, 20, 55-86.

Harris,M., and A.Raviv (1990), Capital Structure and the Informational Role of Debt, Journal of Finance, 45, 321-349.

Harris,M., and A.Raviv (1991), The Theory of Capital Structure, Journal of Finance, 46, 297-355.

Harris,M., and A.Raviv (1992), Financial Contracting Theory, in J.J.Laffont (ed.) Advances in Economic Theory (Cambridge: Cambridge University Press).

Hart,O.D. (1985), Monopolistic Competition in the Spirit of Chamberlin: Special Results, Economic Journal, 75, 889-908.

Heal,G.M., and A.Silberston (1972), Alternative Managerial Objectives: An Explanatory Note, Oxford Economic Papers, 24, 137-150.

Hexter,J.L. (1975), Entropy, Diversification, and the Information Loss Barrier to Entry, Industrial Organization Review, 3, 130-137.

Hicks,J.R. (1935), Annual Survey of Economic Theory: The Theory of Monopoly, Econometrica, 3, 1-20.

Hill,C.W.L. (1984), Organization Structure, the Development of the Firm and Business Behavior, in J.F.Pickering and T.A.J.Cockerill (eds.) The Economic Management of the Firm (Oxford: Phillip Allen).

Hill,C.W.L. (1988), Internal Capital Market Controls and Financial Performance in Multidivisional Firms, Journal of Industrial Economics, 37, 67-83.

Hill,C.W.L., and T.M.Jones (1992), Stakeholder-Agency Theory, Journal of Management Studies, 29, 131-154.

Hill,C.W.L., and J.F.Pickering (1986), Conglomerate Mergers, Internal Organization, and Competition Policy, International Review of Law and Economics, 6, 59-75.

Hitt,M.A., and R.D.Ireland (1986), Relationship Among Corporate Level Distinctive Competencies, Diversification Strategy,

Corporate Structure, and Performance, Journal of Management Studies, 23, 401-416.

Hoenack,S.A. (1983), Economic Behavior Within Organizations (NewYork: Cambridge University Press).

Holstrom,B., and J.Tirole (1989), The Theory of the Firm, in R.Schmalensee and R.D.Willig (eds.) Handbook of Industrial Organization (Amsterdam: Elsevier).

Holt,C.C., F.Modigliani, J.Muth, and H.Simon (1960), Planning Production, Inventory, and the Workforce (Engelwood Cliffs: Prentice Hall).

Ilmakunnas,P. (1985), Bayesian Estimation of Cost Functions with Stochastic or Exact Constraints on Parameters, International Economic Review, 26, 111-134.

Ilmakunnas,P. (1986), Stochastic Constraints on Cost Function Parameters: Mixed and Hierachical Approaches, Empirical Economics, 11, 69-80.

Jensen,M.C., and W.H.Meckling (1976), Theory of the Firm: Managerial Behavior, Agency Costs and Ownership Structure, Journal of Financial Economics, 3, 305-360.

Jensen,M.C., and J.B.Warner (1988), The Distribution of Power Among Corporate Managers, Shareholders, and Directors, Journal of Financial Economics, 20, 3-24.

Jorgensen,S., P.M.Kort, and G.S.van Schijndel (1989), Optimal Investment, Financing, and Dividends, Journal of Economic Dynamics and Control, 13, 339-377.

Kahn,J.A. (1987), Inventories and Volatility of Production, American Economic Review, 77, 667-679.

Kahn,J.A. (1992), Why is Production More Volatile than Sales? Theory and Evidence on the Stockout Motive for Inventory Holding, Quarterly Journal of Economics, 107, 481-510.

Kamecke,U. (1993), The Role of Competition for an X-Inefficiently Organized Firm, International Journal of Industrial Organization, 11, 391-405.

Kashyap,A.K., O.A.Lamont, and J.C.Stein (1994), Credit Conditions and the Cyclical Behavior of Inventories, Quarterly Journal of Economics, 109, 565-592.

Kay,J.A. (1991), Economics and Business, Economic Journal, 101,

57-63.

Kay,J.A. (1995), Foundations of Corporate Success (Oxford: Oxford University Press).

Kay,N. (1984), The Emergent Firm (London: Macmillan).

Kinnie,N. (1987), Bargaining Within the Firm: Centralized or Decentralized?, Journal of Management Studies, 24, 463-477.

Knight,F.H. (1933), The Economic Organization (NewYork: Harper and Row).

Kort,P.M. (1990), Dynamic Firm Behavior within an Uncertain Enviroment, European Journal of Operations Research, 47, 371-386.

Koutsoyiannis,A. (1978), Managerial Job Security and Capital Structure of Firms, Manchester School of Economic and Social Studies, 46, 51-75.

Krane,S.D. (1994), The Distinction Between Inventory Holding and Stockout Costs: Implications for Target Inventories, Asymmetric Adjustment, and the Effect of Aggregation on Production Smoothing, International Economic Review, 35, 117-136.

Langlois,C. (1989), A Model of Target Inventory and Markup with Empirical Testing Using the Automobile Industry Data, Journal of Economic Behavior and Organization, 11, 47-74.

Learned,E.P., C.R.Christensen, K.R.Andrews, and W.D.Guth (1969), Business Policy: Text and Cases (Homewood: Irwin).

Leech,D., and J.Leahy (1991), Ownership Structure, Control Type Classifications and Performance of Large British Companies, Economic Journal, 101, 1418-1437.

Leibenstein,H. (1980), Beyond Economic Man (Cambridge: Harvard University Press).

Levy,D.T., and L.J.Haber (1986), An Advantage of the Multiproduct Firm: The Transferability of Firm Specific Capital, Journal of Economic Behavior and Organization, 7, 291-302.

Lintner,J. (1956), Distribution of Income of Corporations among Dividends, Retained Earnings and Taxes, American Economic Review, 46, 97-113.

Lintner,J. (1971), Optimum or Maximum Corporate Growth Under Uncertainty, in R.Marris and A.Wood (eds.) The Corporate Economy (Cambridge: Harvard University Press).

Lyles,M.A., and C.R.Schwenk (1992), Top Management, Strategy and Organizational Knowledge Structures, Journal of Management Studies, 29, 155-174.

Magnus,J.R., and H.Neudecker (1988), Matrix Differential Calculus (NewYork: Wiley).

Marby,B.D., and D.L.Siders (1967), An Empirical Test of the Sales Maximization Hypothesis, Southern Economic Journal, 3, 367-377.

Marginson,P. (1985), The Multidivisional Firm and Control over the Work Process, International Journal of Industrial Organization, 3, 37-56.

Marris,R. (1964), The Economic Theory of Managerial Capitalism (NewYork: Free Press).

Marris,R. (1971), An Introduction to Theories of Corporate Growth, in R.Marris and A.Wood (eds.) The Corporate Economy (Cambridge: Harvard University Press).

Marshall,W.J., J.B.Yawitz, and E.Greenberg (1984), Incentives for Diversification and the Structure of the Conglomerate Firm, Southern Economic Journal, 51, 1-23.

Mason,R.T. (1971), Executive Motivations, Earnings and Consequent Equity Performace, Journal of Political Economy, 79, 1278-1292.

McConnell,J.J., and C.J.Muscarella (1985), Corporate Capital Expenditure Decisions and the Market Value of the Firm, Journal of Financial Economics, 14, 399-422.

McGuire,J.W., J.S.Y.Chin, and A.O.Elbring (1962), Executive Incomes, Sales, and Profits, American Economic Review, 52, 753-761.

Mester,L.J. (1989), Testing for Expense reference Behavior: Mutual Versus Savings and Loan, Rand Journal of Economics, 20, 483-498.

Miron,J.A., and S.P.Zeldes (1988), Seasonality, Cost Shocks, and the Production Smoothing Model of Inventories, Econometrica, 56, 877-908.

Mueller,D.C. (1967), The Firm Decision Process: An Econometric Investigation, Quarterly Journal of Economics, 81, 58-87.

Mueller,D.C. (1986), Profits in the Long Run (Cambridge: Cambridge University Press).

Murphy,K.J. (1985), Corporate Performance and Managerial Remuneration: An Empirical Analysis, Journal of Accounting and

Economics, 7, 11-42.

Myers,S. (1984), The Capital Structure Puzzle, Journal of Finance, 39, 575-592.

Naish,H.F. (1994), Production Smoothing in the Linear Quadratic Inventory Model, Economic Journal, 104, 864-875.

Nelson,P. (1975), The Economic Consequences of Advertising, Journal of Business, 48, 213-245.

Netter,J.M. (1982), Excessive Advertising: An Empirical Analysis, Journal of Industrial Economics, 30, 361-373.

Nyman,S., and A.Silberston (1978), The Ownership and Control of Industry, Oxford Economic Papers, 30, 74-101.

Ouchi,W.G. (1984), The M-Form Society (NewYork: Addison Wesley).

Penrose,E.T. (1959), The Theory of the Growth of the Firm (NewYork: Wiley).

Phillips,A. (1962), Market Structure, Organization, and Performance (Cambridge: Harvard University Press).

Phlips,L. (1983), The Economics of Price Discrimination (Cambridge: Cambridge University Press).

Pindyck,R.S. (1994), Inventories and the Short-Run Dynamics of Commodity Prices, Rand Journal of Economics, 25, 141-159.

Porter,M.E. (1981), The Contributions of Industrial Organization to Strategic Management, Academy of Management Review, 6, 609-620.

Radice,H.K. (1971), Control Type, Profitability and Growth in Large Firms, Economic Journal, 81, 547-562.

Rao,C.R. (1965), Linear Statistical Inference and its Applications (NewYork: Wiley).

Rao,T.V.S.R. (1988 a), Demand Uncertainty, Decision Models of the Firm, and Parameter Estimation, Journal of Quantitative Economics, 4, 45-58.

Rao,T.V.S.R. (1988 b), Econometric Estimation of Decision Models Under Uncertainty, in J.K.Sengupta and G.K.Kadekodi (eds.) Econometrics of Planning and Efficiency (Dordrecht: Kluwer Academic Publishers).

Rao,T.V.S.R. (1989), Economic Efficiency of the Organizational Decisions of the Firm (Heidelberg: Springer Verlag).

Rao,T.V.S.R. (1991 a), NEIO: Some Often Neglected Aspects of

Specification and Inference, Arthavijnana, 33, 159-174.

Rao,T.V.S.R. (1991 b), Financial Choices of the Firm as Organizational Decisions, International Review of Economics and Business, 38, 753-778.

Rao,T.V.S.R. (1991 c), Inventories and Welfare, International Review of Economics and Business, 38, 267-287.

Rao,T.V.S.R. (1993), Contracts: Effects on Resource Allocation and Economic Welfare, Indian Journal of Economics, 73, 489-512.

Rao,T.V.S.R. (1994), Estimating Attitudes Towards Risk in a Volatile Environment, Indian Journal of Applied Economics, 3, 253-270.

Rao,T.V.S.R., and R.Rastogi (1995 a), Managerial Preferences for Holding Inventory, Indian Journal of Applied Economics, 4, 27-53.

Rao,T.V.S.R., and R.Rastogi (1995 b), Identification of Managerial Preferences, to be presented at the India and Asia meetings of the Econometric Society, New Delhi, 1996.

Rao,T.V.S.R., and R.Rastogi (1996), Excessive Selling Costs: An Alternative Formulation, Unpublished manuscript.

Rao,T.V.S.R., R.Rastogi, and S.Saha (1995), Capital Structure Decision: Implicit Contract or a Governance Relation?, International Review of Economics and Business, 42, 145-162.

Rao,T.V.S.R., and S.Saha (1994 a), Interactive Effects of Organizational Structure and Control on Corporate Performance, Journal of Quantitative Economics, 10, 293-308.

Rao,T.V.S.R., and S.Saha (1994 b), Business Policy and Corporate Performance, Indian Economic Journal, 42, 39-53.

Rao,T.V.S.R., and R.Sharma (1984), Primacy of Corporate Dividend Decisions, Indian Economic Journal, 32, 56-72.

Rao,T.V.S.R., and S.P.Singh (1987), Demand Uncertainty, Price Fixing Firms, and Parameter Estimation, Economic Letters, 24, 243-247.

Rao,T.V.S.R., and S.P.Singh (1990 a), CORE: For Decision Models Under Uncertainty, Economics Letters, 34, 43-48.

Rao,T.V.S.R., and S.P.Singh (1990 b), CORE Vs. MLE for Decision Models Under Uncertainty, Zeitschrift fur Nationalokonomie, 51, 145-158.

Rao,T.V.S.R., S.P.Singh, and P.P.Talwar (1991 a), Estimation and Structure of Price-Cost Margins Under Uncertainty, Advances in Econometrics, 9, 61-85.

Rao,T.V.S.R., S.P.Singh, and P.P.Talwar (1991 b), Decisions of the Firm Under Uncertainty: Estimation and Structure of Price-Cost Margins, International Review of Economics and Business, 38, 355-368.

Rastogi,R., and T.V.S.R.Rao (1995), Corporate Governance and Capital Structure, Presented at the 1996 Indian Econometric Society meetings in Bangalore.

Ravid,S.A., and E.F.Sudit (1994), Power Seeking Managers, Profitable Dividends, and Financing Decisions, Journal of Economic Behavior and Organization, 25, 241-255.

Rediker,K.J., and A.Seth (1995), Boards of Directors and Substitution Effects of Alternative Governance Mechanisms, Strategic Management Journal, 15, 85-99.

Rothenberg,T.J. (1971), Identification in Parametric Models, Econometrica, 39, 577-592.

Rozeff,M.S. (1982), Growth, Beta and Agency Costs as Determinants of Dividend Payout Ratios, Journal of Financial Research, 5, 249-259.

Rubin,L. (1979), Aggregate Inventory Behavior: Response to Uncertainty and Interest Rates, Journal of Post Keynesian Economics, 2, 201-211.

Santere,R., and S.Neun (1986), Stock Dispersion and Executive Compensation, Review of Economics and Statistics, 68, 685-687.

Sass,T.R., and D.S.Saurman (1995), Advertising Restrictions and Concentration: The Case of Malt Beverages, Review of Economics and Statistics, 77, 66-81.

Schmalensee,R. (1978), Entry Deterrence in Ready-to-Eat Breakfast Cereal Industry, Bell Journal of Economics, 9, 305-327.

Schmalensee,R. (1988), Industrial Economics: An Overview, Economic Journal, 98, 643-681.

Schmalensee,R. (1989), Inter-Industry Studies of Structure and Performance, in R.Schmalensee and R.D.Willig (eds.) Handbook of Industrial Organization (Amsterdam: Elsevier Science Publishers).

Sengupta,J.K. (1988), Efficiency Analysis by Production Frontiers:

The Nonparametric Approach (Dordrecht: Kluwer Academic Publishers).

Sengupta,J.K. (1995), Dynamics of Data Envelopment Analysis (Dordrecht: Kluwer Academic Publishers).

Sharkey,W.W. (1982), The Theory of Natural Monopoly (Cambridge: Cambridge University Press).

Skilvas,S.D. (1987), The Strategic Choice of Managerial Incentives, Rand Journal of Economics, 18, 452-458.

Smith, C.W., and R.L.Watts (1992), The Investment opportunity Set and Corporate Financing, Dividend, and Compensation Policies, Journal of Financial Economics, 32, 263-292.

Spence,M. (1977), Nonprice Competition, American Economic Review, 67, 255-259.

Stultz,R.M. (1990), Managerial Discretion and Optimal Financing Policies, Journal of Financial Economics, 26 3-28.

Teece,D.J. (1980), Economies of Scope and the Scope of the Enterprise, Journal of Economic Behavior and Organization, 1, 237-247.

Tirole,J. (1988), The Theory of Industrial Organization (Cambridge: M.I.T.Press).

Turnovsky,S.J. (1970), Financial Structure and the Theory of Production, Journal of Finance, 25, 1061-1080.

Utton,M.A. (1982), The political Economy of Big Business (Oxford: Martin Robertson).

Varadarajan,P.R., and V.Ramanujam (1990), The Corporate Performance Conundrum: A Synthesis of Contemporary Views and an Extension, Journal of Management Studies, 27, 463-484.

Vickers,D. (1968), The Theory of the Firm: Production, Capital, and Finance (NewYork: McGraw Hill).

Vickers,D. (1987), Money Capital in the Theory of the Firm (Cambridge: Cambridge University Press).

Walter,J.E. (1963), Dividend Policy: Its Influence on the Value of the Enterprise, Journal of Finance, 18, 280-291.

Wanvani,A. (1993), The Hierarchy Busters, Business World, 15-28 December, 106-107.

Ware,R. (1985), Inventory Holding as a Strategic Weapon to Deter Entry, Economica, 52, 93-102.

Weiss,L.W., G.Pascoe, and S.Martin (1988), The Size of Selling Costs, Review of Economics and Statistics, 65, 668-672.

Welch,R.L. (1980), Vertical and Horizontal Communication in Economic Processes, Review of Economic Studies, 47, 733-746.

West.K.D. (1988), Order Backlogs and Production Smoothing, in A.Chikan and M.Lowell (eds.) The Economics of Inventory Management (Amsterdam: Elsevier Science Publishers).

Whittington,R. (1988), Structure and Theories of Strategic Choice, Journal of Management Studies, 25, 521-536.

Williams,J. (1987), Perquisites, Risk, and Capital Structure, Journal of Finance, 42, 29-49.

Williamson,O.E. (1964), The Economics of Discretionary Behavior: Managerial Objectives in a Theory of the Firm (Englewood Cliffs: Prentice Hall).

Williamson,O.E. (1971), Managerial Discretion, Organizational Form, and the Multidivision Hypothesis, in R.Marris and A.Wood (eds.) The Corporate Economy (London: Macmillan).

Williamson,O.E., (1986), The Multidivisional Structure, in J.B.Barney and W.G.Ouchi (eds.) Organizational Economics (SanFransisco: Jossey Bass).

Williamson,O.E. (1988), Corporate Finance and Corporate Governance, Journal of Finance, 43, 567-591.

Wintrobe,R., and A.Breton (1986), Organizational Structure and Productivity, American Economic Review, 76, 530-538.

Wolak,F.A. (1989 a), Local and Global Testing of Linear and Nonlinear Inequality Constraints in Nonlinear Economic Models, Econometric Theory, 5, 1-35.

Wolak,F.A. (1989 b), Testing Inequality Constraints in Linear Economic Models, Journal of Econometrics, 41, 205-235.

Yarrow,G.K. (1973), Managerial Utility Maximization Under Uncertainty, Economica, 40, 155-173.

Yarrow,G.K. (1976), On the Predictions of Managerial Theories of the Firm, Journal of Industrial Economics, 24, 267-279.

Young,A.A. (1928), Increasing Returns and Business Progress, Economic Journal, 38, 527-542.

INDEX